Slightly off

the Mark

THE UNPUBLISHED COLUMNS

by Mark R. Hunter

Other titles by Mark

Romantic comedy
Storm Chaser
The Notorious Ian Grant

Non-fiction
Smoky Days and Sleepless Nights: A Century or So with the Albion Fire Department
Images of America: Albion and Noble County (August 2015)

Novellas and Short Stories
The No-Campfire Girls
Storm Chaser Shorts

Edited by Emily J. Hunter

Design, cover, and contributions by Emily J. Hunter

Any opinions given within are those of the author only, although he secretly thinks everyone agrees with him, and any information given is correct to the best of the author's knowledge. Mistakes are not intentional, as is usually the case with mistakes. No small animals were harmed in the making of this work, and the author was harmed only a little.

DEDICATION

I did it for the lolz.

Well, it was nice to get paid for writing, too. But mostly I did it for the most selfish reason at all: For that rush of happiness that comes with making people laugh. I did it for all the readers, most in northeast Indiana but many in other states, and sometimes in other countries. I did it to make them laugh, which made me happy, so I suppose in the end I did it for me.

This work, then, is dedicated to all the readers of my column for twenty-three years, especially those who have voiced their appreciation, and their upset when "Slightly Off The Mark" lost its home. It's in a monthly paper now, the Kendallville Mall, but also here between the pages of a book; I hope it will be warm and comfortable here, and well-fed by readers in a not-horror movie kind of way.

Slightly off
the Mark

THE UNPUBLISHED COLUMNS

PART ONE:

because someone has to go first

Some writers are good at beginnings, some are good at endings, and a few are good at middles. I'm good at dialogue. Since there's not much dialogue in non-fiction, I chose how to start this book the scientific way: I threw all my columns in the air, chose a dozen, and bob's your uncle. I'm not suggesting you actually have an uncle named Bob— it's just an expression from my British friends. But if you do, that's just fine.

Apparently "Bob's your uncle" means something to the effect of "it's very simple", which, now that I think of it, is a bit insulting. There's also a Canadian band named Bob's Your Uncle which, ironically, has no one named Bob in it. I'm way too lazy to find out if any of the members have an Uncle Bob.

(In no way does this intend to demean or insult Bob, or Canadians, although I can't make any guarantees about future volumes.)

WHY I WRITE, OR: I HATE NEEDLES

Many years ago, the editor at the newspaper where I worked part time gave me an opportunity that only comes once, the chance so many writers beg for: They offered me a column of my very own.

I said no.

It wasn't the first or last time I passed up on great opportunities, and it wasn't until years later, when I was diagnosed with Seasonal Affected Disorder, that I realized why. The offer had come to me in late January, the best possible time for people with SAD to retreat from the world and form little fetal positions inside their kitchen ovens. How many of us, people with that rare intelligence who understand winter is horrible and should be slept through, lost out on great chances because they weren't willing to wade through snow drifts to get a diagnosis?

I had started out providing my home town's weekly newspaper with press releases from our local volunteer fire department and EMS service. Eventually they hired me to send in news items, and at some point somebody there thought I might be capable of writing 52,000 funny words a year.

I blew it. But, in a burst of rare winter smarts, I turned around a few minutes later, walked into the *Albion New Era* office with the aura of confidence and skill, and said, "I changed my mind. Pleasssseeeee!!!!!!"

Over the next twenty years I raised two kids, got a divorce, started a new job, got remarried, and eventually published three novels, a collection of short stories, and a non-fiction history book. During all that time—from early February of 1991 until last week, which according to my watch was October 16, 2014, I wrote my weekly column. It was printed in three local newspapers, and on my blog ... a blog being something no one had any idea was coming in 1991.

There were those occasions when I got lazy and went for a reprint, and one or two times when circumstances forced my column out of the paper. Still, a thousand words a pop adds up to some one million, one hundred and fifty thousand words.

That's written out as 1,150,000 words. That's as if, instead of publishing my first novel, I published nineteen first novels.

No wonder I'm tired.

But just as things can rise quickly, they can fall quickly, except the Federal debt. On October 9 I picked up the newspaper and learned it had been sold. Exactly one week later I received a phone call from one of the head buying people, informing me that I had become a "duplication of services". I was the victim of corporate downsizing.

But I've been in this business a long time, and I've been poor before, and besides, I still had a full time job. I picked myself up and forged ahead, not at the exact same time, because I couldn't forge ahead *while* picking myself up. Brimming with confidence, I ...

Not buying it, eh? Okay, I broke down into a sniveling pile of fear and uncertainty. Satisfied? My wife was very supportive, although the dog seemed disgusted by my whimpering.

But I did pick myself up, because there's no profitability in sniveling piles unless you play one on TV. I have a face made for radio, and a voice made for writing. I had two choices: sell plasma, or keep writing.

I hate needles.

Now, if I'm anything, I'm a writer, and if I'm anything else, I'm a font of insecurities. (I tried once to be a font of comic sans, but my wife slapped that down real fast.) Deadlines taught me to write on—well, on deadline, but they also made me more stressed than Charlie Sheen's probation officer. Whenever a vacation approached, I'd write two or three columns ahead of time, just in case I got too busy making merry. Whenever winter approached, I'd write four or five columns ahead of time, just in case I got too busy with the exact opposite of making merry. For the first time, my SAD became an advantage: I counted up my unpublished columns, and came up with more than thirty.

And here they are, along with some more new material and maybe a few older classic columns, depending on whether I forgot they got printed back in the pre-internet days. Now, I don't know what will be going on by the time you read this. Maybe I'll have another column somewhere else; maybe I'll be an adman in Chicago; maybe I'll be writing assembly instructions for IKEA. But I'll still be writing, and if enough people like this book, you can be sure you'll see another one.

(Update: As I finish this my column is now in the monthly Kendallville Mall, *and I just finished a photo history book about Albion and Noble County.)*

Until then, this is my gift to you, my readers, who were supportive of my effort and honestly sad and angry when it came to an abrupt end. And when I say gift, keep in mind you still have to pay for it, so stop sliding this copy toward your purse. Sheesh.

CLASSING UP THE JOINT

I can't think of a better way to start than to introduce my wife/webmaster/editor/business manager/technical consultant/dog handler, who's so much smarter than me that averaged between us our IQ is normal. We met on a writing related website, and for weeks Emily thought I was female; to this day, she still says I write like a girl. Well, I've written two romantic comedies, so it's hard to argue that. In any case, it's no wonder she went to college, and I just drove by one.

After graduating from high school, I moved into an efficiency apartment in the middle of Albion, Indiana. Although it's a small town, everything I had any interest in (except women) was within walking distance: My writing, the fire station, the EMS quarters, the library, and work. Pretty much in that order.

The apartment was slightly smaller than my '76 Pontiac Ventura, but contained what I needed: a table just large enough to hold my manual typewriter, a stack of scrap paper with one clean side, and a dictionary. The rest would be history, and someday there'd be a little plaque on the front door (okay, the only door) of that one room salute to literary beginnings.

Years later, after I'd moved on and my writing career hadn't, the building burned down.

Boy, I wish I'd gone to college.

But after marrying a college student, I'm not at all certain I could hack the college life. I loved being there (there in this case being the Indiana University-Purdue University campus in Fort Wayne), but it was easy for me because I didn't have to take any classes. I could just live on that campus and never leave. I mean, it's got a library, a coffee shop, and fast food joints – what else would a writer need?

On the other hand, every time finals come around I wonder who'd be crazy enough to tackle a full college degree.

I went to the school of hard knocks. I had to walk ten miles through life every day, uphill both ways, in a raging blizzard in the morning and a parched dust storm in the afternoon. And I was darned glad to have the black paint we used to cover our feet because we couldn't afford shoes.

But it couldn't have been worse than collage finals.

My wife is a type A student who went to every class if she could move at all, actually read the books, and genuinely enjoys learning. And yet, for two weeks at the end of every semester she went into a crisis mode that makes the crew of Apollo 13 look like a bunch of slackers. I can't imagine how more casual students manage to make it through one semester, let alone graduate. I keep picturing bewildered students at the end of the year, stumbling into each other in the hallways and moaning, "I thought it would be like high school!"

It's not.

I've taken some college level courses, in the area of the emergency services and writing; I even took a course at IPFW once. But it was one class at a time. There are young people who work full time, go to college full time, don't get fired, and keep their grades up. I don't know how. Cloning?

On the other hand, my school of hard knocks has taken me a few decades, and my degree in B.S. is–believe me–not the same one you pick up in college. In fact, the School of Hard Knocks (SOK), is like being a parent in that you never really stop, never really know if you succeeded, and never graduate. At least Emily got a degree.

But first she had to get through the work load, which is compressed into a tighter time period than getting SOK'd around. Not only do you have to work hard in the classes that interest you, but you have to pass all the required and elective stuff that *doesn't* interest you. Math would have been ten times the problem for me than it would be for others. Maybe twenty times. I don't know. Twenty-five?

There's some relief for students who take electives, those easy classes that you can coast through to improve your GPA. Here are some examples:

"Cross-Cultural Perspectives, Analysis, and Evaluation – of Daytime Soap Operas."

"A Metaphor Of Etruscan Symbols: Exploration Of Suicide In Australian Poetry"

"The Consequences Of Latvian Scientists On 21st Century Extraterrestrial Biology: A Paradigm Shift."

"The Influence Of Mayan Poetry On Modern Liberal Evolution: A Paradigm Shift."

(There's an awfully lot of paradigm shifting going on in college, isn't there? Sometimes, if your paradigm shifts too much, you need surgery.)

And, of course, the classic: Underwater Basket Weaving. That's a real class, by the way. And you may think it's easy, but have you ever tried to weave a basket underwater? I can't even open my eyes underwater. When I took the class, I stabbed two classmates and the teacher. You don't get passed when that happens.

Eventually, if you're lucky and work hard, you get to finals week – which I've learned is closer to two weeks, or longer if you try to prepare. Some of Emily's finals were projects, which if done right take more time than the test, *and* studying for the test. On most of her finals there was a dreaded *essay question*. True and false? For the weak. Here are some examples of college level questions:

"During the period from 1492 to 1700, French activity in the Americas was primarily directed toward:"

Um ... surrendering?

"The sum of the two roots of a quadratic equation is 5 and their product is -6. Which of the following could be the equation?"

Forty-two. Yep.

"As rain mixes with chemicals such as sulfur dioxide in the air, acid rain is produced. This may result in:"

Zombies.

"Die Kinder gehen zum . . . , um frische Brötchen zu kaufen."

Jeez, that one's like a whole different language!

So, don't let anyone tell you college is easy – at least, not if you want that sheepskin. In the end, having a sheep involved in your education is a lot more worthwhile than the bull that came with my B.S. degree.

I LOVE LEARNING, BUT DON'T TEST ME ON THAT

This shows what I'm all about as a columnist: mentioning weather, making fun of serious stuff, and less than subtle plugs for my books. The only thing left is an injury while attempting home maintenance.

Now that I'm out of school and don't have to take tests anymore, I love learning. That would freak some people out, I suppose – far too many take the end of school as an excuse to stop learning, unless they're learning the latest contestant to be dropped from The Biggest Losing Apprentice Housewife Chefs of New Jersey Shores.

I suppose part of it is that whole book-writing thing. A lot of time goes into a non-fiction book: When I was researching my history of the fire department, I spent enough time at the library to qualify for retirement. But you'd be surprised how much research goes into novels, too. The young adult mystery I finished a few years ago required me to learn about police and private detective work, Native American history, firefighting (well, I kinda already knew that), and how an amusement park operates behind the scenes.

All that for a story I "made up".

Storm Chaser required a good working knowledge of meteorology, because, hey – storms. (It turns out meteorology is *not* the study of meteors. That's called, ironically, Rock-rainology.)

Like many people in Indiana, I already had some working knowledge of weather. It's a survival thing:

"Hey, it's 80 degrees and sunny out!"

"Take your coat."

"But it's 80 degrees and – where did that cloud come from? Is that – snow?"

"It's March. Take your coat, and some sunscreen, and a life jacket."

As a storm spotter I'd also learned certain things: Harmless scud clouds mean people are going to call 911 and report a tornado on the ground. Quarter sized hail hurts. The tornado siren is a statewide signal for everyone to go stand in their front yard.

Still, when you write a character who makes her living following disasters around the country, you'd better have some of the same knowledge she does. Despite my already well known fascination with The Weather Channel, I learned as much as I could about meteorology without actually taking a class. (They charge for those. Who knew?)

I fudged a little on the opening of the book, because I inserted a tornado into weather conditions that probably couldn't produce one. (It's not a spoiler – that's quite literally how the book opens.) Still, I had to know the rules in order to even consider breaking them, just as I had to know the rules of a good story – including the one about getting the reader's attention with page one. Tornadoes are notorious attention grabbers.

Now, I told you all that so you'll understand why I was bothered by a catalog I received in the mail. My wife, who I'll call Emily because that's her name, is just as fascinated by learning as I am, and together we ordered a couple of DVD classes from a company called "The Great Courses".

You people who hate learning, you'd better brace yourselves for this.

Simply put, The Great Courses allows you to order an illustrated lecture series – in a sense, you're taking a college course in your own home, only without being tested or graded. Also, without getting college credit ... there's always a catch.

In other words, we were learning just for the sake of learning. Somebody get chairs for those drop-outs in the back row, who are swooning at the very thought.

There are courses on history, science, literature, even math. There will be no math in my home, by the way – you gotta draw the line somewhere. The courses we ordered had to do with history and writing. Remember that.

Okay, so I've set it up for you. We ordered two courses, which of course resulted in a flood of catalogs from the company. It's a tactic that would have done what they desired if I had the money: I'd hold up in my living room, watching DVD's, all winter. Since I don't have the money, I'm writing a column instead.

Ah, well. The catalogs were a kind of torture, but interesting to browse through and useful for kindling material for January, just in case the worst-case scenario comes along. Then, one day, a new catalog came in that caused me to stop in my tracks.

Naturally, the companies have a customer list and will personalize their categories, I understand that. But this one was a bit too personal, especially since they knew nothing about me except my name and address:

"Mark, we've placed a course on sale especially for you! Order now and take $15 off the sale price of:

"Meteorology."

Um .....

Okay, so I wrote a novel about a meteorologist/storm chaser, and the weather plays a key part of the story. But – how they heck did they know that? It's not like they shot me a personalized cover every week with a different subject on it, just to cover all their bases.

What next? Will my fire history book put me on the mailing list for *Fire Chief Magazine?* Will my mystery net an internal memo at the FBI? Will my anti-Congress columns get me blacklisted by Harry Reid and John Boehner?

Actually, I'd probably brag about that last one.

INSULTING CHARLIE ROSE

Researchers now say action movies make you fat.

I don't think anyone's really surprised by any of this. We're not surprised that yet another thing is declared to be bad for us. We're not surprised sitting in a chair with a 55 gallon drum of heavily buttered popcorn makes us fat. We're not surprised someone— probably from a "Department of" something— financed this research.

I'm a little surprised that the type of movie matters.

The researchers used college students, with one group watching the movie "The Island", another watching the same clip from that movie without sound (?) and the third watching an interview on "Charlie Rose".

I guess the theory is that "Charlie Rose" is something of a snooze fest, and so not as distracting to the watchers, and we all know college students are hard to distract. Personally, I would have thought they'd eat more when less distracted. Wouldn't they think about food, instead of the screen?

It turns out the opposite was true. With or even without sound, the action movie watchers snacked more than the undistracted group. The researchers concluded that the distraction of the action scene was the key factor—they ate without thinking about it. "Even without sound, you could still get higher levels of engagement" said the study leader, Aner Tal of Cornell.

Which seems kind of insulting to Charlie Rose. Maybe he was having one of his less exciting guests on.

A previous study supposedly showed that moviegoers would get so engrossed by the movie that they'd even eat stale popcorn. But did anyone check to see if that study was made in Canada? Maybe they were just really polite.

Here's another possibility: "The Island" is a Michael Bay motion picture. His movies tend to be so over the top as to be ridiculous. Is it possible the moviegoers were so disgusted with what they were watching that they were just trying to get their money's worth of snacks? I mean, the last third of "Armageddon" was an almost incomprehensible mix of fast cuts and explosions—I thought the film was jumping like an old record.

One must also, even outside of Canada, take politeness into consideration.

Here's what I mean: Maybe, when they were playing the version of "The Island" without sound, people started snacking just because the silence was starting to bother them.

Another possibility is that with an action film, polite people were binge snacking. I do that: If I wanted some popcorn during "Guardians Of The Galaxy", I'd stuff handfuls into my mouth during the battle sequences. Why? Because I didn't want to bother people with the sound of chewing during the quieter moments.

Yes, I turn my cell phone off, too.

Okay, that's not the likely explanation, considering how unfailingly impolite people seem to have become. Let's turn to how we should solve the problem. Watch fewer movies?

I don't think so. Especially not now, when my favorite superheroes are finally getting some loving on the big screen. (Not literally—ew.)

How about this: Don't have as many snacks in front of you. Crazy, huh? If you have to leave the theater, or even if you have to hit pause to head into the kitchen, you're less likely to over snack.

Common sense strikes again!

What's going to happen next is pretty clear. Michelle Obama will lead an officially sanctioned government charge against action films. Lawsuits by obese moviegoers going through yet another bypass surgery will pour in. New laws will limit the length of an action film, then the percentage and intensity of action scenes.

A push will be on to limit sizes of all containers in movie theaters, with popcorn and soda no longer coming in extra-anything. TV—of all places—will introduce a new after school special, about a middle school kid who snacks so much during "Expendables 4: Washed Up Again" that he gets stuck, and has to be pried out of his movie seat with the Jaws Of Life. Michael Moore will begin campaigning for bigger theater seats, while shooting his documentary: "Fatwa Like Me—America's Real Enemy".

In addition to the forty minutes of trailers and ads we already see, there will be legally mandated slides before each movie, telling us the average number of calories we're likely to gain based on estimated from the newest Federal agency, the Department of Motion Picture Obesity, headed by Secretary of Fat Michael Bloomberg.

Armed with still more evidence that Americans can't take care of themselves, the Federal Government will get … wait for it … fatter.

The danger is growing.

STRESSING OUT OVER STRESS REDUCTION

The fabled Fountain of Youth really exists, if you know where to look. Many think it's in Florida, but consider the number of people with white hair in that state.

No: The Fountain of Youth is on the internet.

The other day, for no good reason other than avoiding work, I Googled "10 Ways to Stay Young" and got 175,000,000 responses. There you go: The internet keeps you young.

The first suggestion, ironically, was to *avoid work.*

Specifically it was to give yourself a break from stress, which is pretty much the same thing. Up to 90% of doctor visits are related to anxiety, depression, anger, or hostility, or so I told my doctor as I threw things at him while trying to jump out of his office window.

The suggested solution was meditation, something I've heard before, and that's when it hit me: I need to counter these with 10 ways to stay young in the real world. So I made a few changes to the solutions:

Give yourself a break.

Meditate ... with a good book. If you can't find a good book, you're not looking hard enough. I would suggest romance, science fiction, or fantasy. And not that post apocalyptical depressing everyone dies in the end science fiction, either. Or maybe that would be perfect: "Look how good my life is compared to being eaten by mutant zombies while dying of radiation poisoning!" There is that.

If you absolutely refuse to read – well, you don't know what you're missing. But watch a movie based on a book instead, while keeping this in mind: The book was better.

You could also take a hot bath, with soft music and candles and stuff. Try to keep the book dry.

Consume more fat.

That's what I'm talkin' about.

Specifically, Omega-3 fatty acids help mood, and bone strength, and reduce inflammation. You can get it from nuts. However, I've found that having too many nuts around increases my stress levels. Here's my suggestion:

Stock up on ice cream, candy bars, and barbecue flavored potato chips. Go to the list of ingredients. Find a black marker, and wherever you see "fat", write "Omega-3". Enjoy, preferably while reading in the bathtub. Try not to get the food wet.

Get off the couch.

This is a reasonable suggestion, as exercise has many health benefits. Here's my suggestion: Walk to the grocery store. Get some ice cream, candy bars, and potato chips. Now, here's the key: Do *not* go back and eat them on the couch.

Instead, walk straight into the bathroom, exercising on the way by pulling off your clothes and picking up a book. While reading and snacking in the bathtub, move your legs around for exercise. Keep the water hot, as this will help sweat out the non-Omega fatty acids.

"Feel the love."

They mean embrace life: Take up new hobbies, join a book club, do whatever makes you feel energized and alive, like eating chocolate. This section also covers that great exercise, sex. The best kind is loving sex, according to Doctor Oz, who usually practices in the Emerald City but also covers veterinary and pediatrics in the Munchkin Country.

There's an ongoing rumor that Doctor Oz is also the Wizard of Oz, what with rumors that they're both humbugs. But the main point remains: Banish boredom and isolation at all costs.

My solution: Get a bigger bathtub. If you can't afford that, don't let love in the shower make you feel all dirty.

Drink Red Wine.

When a mouse's diet is supplemented with a substance found on the skin of grapes it tends to live longer, unless I catch it in my kitchen. A little red wine can diminish stroke damage, reduce artery clogging and cholesterol, and get you in the mood for that bigger bathtub. However, notice that every single article that mentions red wine also mentions the term "a *little*".

My solution? Well, you and your significant other need something to wash down the chips and barbeque ribs, right? (I mention ribs because they're messy, and you're already in the bathtub, anyway.)

Yoga.

I find yoga to be maddeningly impossible, until I came up with a solution: Avoid any yoga pose you can't do in the bathtub, while reading and holding a candy bar. That takes a lot of the stress out of it.

Eat Superfruit.

Fruits such as pomegranates and goji berry have incredible anti-aging benefits. However, experts caution, get the goji berries from Tibet, which have extra high levels of the good stuff that I can't pronounce.

My take? It's a scam perpetuated by the Tibetan Agricultural Board. There are berries in red wine—go to town, and add in some candy bars with fruit in them. Or have sangria, which has all sorts of fruit, but also medicinal wine and very medicinal brandy.

Also, any green soda has fruit flavor that fools your body into getting healthy out of fear that you'll turn to goji berries.

Drink green tea.

Green tea reduces the risk of breast cancer and maybe other cancers, helps with weight management, keeps your brain sharp, and goes well with chips and ribs, and almost anything else barbecued.

My solution: Mix green tea with red wine in the bathtub. I mean while you're in the bathtub – don't pour it into the bathtub. Or maybe that would help the skin. On a related note:

Put lots of supplements on your skin.

Various products can smooth skin and prevent wrinkles, giving skin the kind of general radiance you usually only find in highly radiated post-apocalyptical landscapes. Some include retinol, alpha lipoic acid, and madecassol.

My solution: You're in the bathtub anyway. If you can figure out what that stuff is, pour it in!

Finally: *Do mental aerobics.*

Hey, you have to figure out how to fill a bathtub with skin cream and red wine, then bathe in the company of at least one other person with a snack in one hand and a book in the other, without getting the snack or the book wet.

How much more mental exercise do you need?

Interstitial One

To show my love for humanity, I'm putting an extra special original segment in between each part of this book. Do any humorists really love humanity? Wouldn't that erase much of their source material?

No, I'm actually doing it because so many of my extra columns published here are commentaries on the world, or internet things, or writing about writing. I figure, a lot of people signed on from the beginning to find out about what silly things were going on in my life, right? Right? So not only do you get to read columns no one has ever read, you get to read stuff between the columns that no one has ever read, and I just realized it's really not all that special.

IT'S ALL ABOUT THE DOG

Our dog weighs about 90 pounds and is around four or five years old, but still thinks he's a puppy. In this, he's not too unlike most men.

We don't know exactly how old Bae is; he was found wandering around the countryside about an hour's drive from our home, trying to pick up female dogs. The vet he was taken to cured him of that desire. The only other thing we know about him is that half his weight is in regularly replaced fur.

Generally I don't mind Bae acting like a big kid, because it gets some of the pressure off me to act my age. (By the way, his full name is Baeowulf, a purposeful misspelling so we can say his nickname. The original Beowulf of myth was a big hairy guy who stole food off plates and pooped in the backyard, so you can see the similarity.)

There are advantages to having a dog who thinks he's a few years younger and a few dozen pounds smaller. For instance, we can play on the floor together and nobody thinks anything of it. The average person would get quite the reputation if they rolled around on the floor by themselves. It looks a little scary, though, because when we start playing his teeth come out, and the unacquainted stranger would likely run away yelling "rabid wolf! And there's a dog, too!"

Since we really aren't kids, we also spend a lot of time lying on the floor, panting until we're rested enough to get up. In fact, we'd both rather sleep sixteen hours a day, although he manages it more often than I do.

There are also disadvantages to youthful thinking dogs. He sleeps a lot, but he never sleeps deeply: Bae is serious about his job, which is guarding the house—especially the boss of the house, who he has interpreted as being my wife. If all three of us are together on a walk, he's anxious to meet people and get petted. If only the two of them are out together, he's anxious to tear your arm off.

That part I'm okay with, but he can't quite understand the concept of the house being securely locked. Did I mention he never sleeps deeply? If someone shuts their car door across the street at the bank, he'll be down the stairs and howling at the front door before you can say "Wha—huh?" which is what I usually say when I'm sleeping. I sleep more deeply than he does. When I'm awake, it's usually "Quiet!"

"Quiet" is dog for "bark louder".

But that is his job, after all. No, the worst thing about him being a 90 pound puppy is the way he dismounts furniture, and the way he gets my attention. We only allow him on the couch, and every now and then on the bed if it's a three dog night, or if he's being bothered by lightning or bad dreams. He whimpers when he has bad dreams—probably nightmares about evil cats, or the vet who made him not care about female dogs.

When it's time to get up, no matter which end of the couch or side of the bed, he always bounds over me. One paw always seems to put his full weight on one place, like he's a guided crotch missile. Yeah, that's right.

And his aim is unerring.

The same thing happens when he wants my attention. Oh, he thinks he's putting his little puppy paw on my knee. What he's really doing is planting one of those ham-sized mitts right on the things he doesn't have any more. It happens so fast, all I can do is curl into a ball and make a whine louder than any he could hope to come up with, even in a whole room of vets.

It's just ... nuts.

Or maybe he's just jealous.

I'm guarding the mistress, so bring that hand a little closer ... I'm hungry.

PART DEUX:

The final second

I have no particular reason to put a section break here. It's just that this section was twice as long as the other sections, and that bugged me.

The truth is, there's no reason to put in section breaks at all—the columns all have their own titles, after all. Who cares how you get there? It's like having to show your work in math class. Boy, that sure takes me to some dark memories.

So, yeah, I'm a little ashamed that I let the section break thing get to me, and you're suffering for it. Please don't tell my parents I was this inconsiderate. You might as well go ahead and tell my wife—she'd editing this book, so I suspect she'll find out [Editor's note: She did].

I'D LIKE TO REMAIN ANONYMOUS ABOUT ME

If you get offended when people give their honest opinion of you, don't give them a chance to do so anonymously.

Pretty good, huh? I'm thinking of having that one put on a bumper sticker.

Facebook had a quiz in which people could answer questions about you, and you wouldn't find out who unless you give your own opinions of other people. Yes, it's just as silly as it sounds.

I didn't give it much thought, because I don't have the time or inclination to opine on, for instance, whether my Facebook friends sleep with a teddy bear. However, I stumbled across an entire list of the answers my FB friends gave – about me.

My day went downhill from there.

Now, I don't know who gave these answers, for reasons previously mentioned, but some of them were pretty brave considering I *could* find out. Let's take a look, and I'll even provide some answers.

I do not still sleep with a teddy bear. One person said yes to this, and one no – hopefully it wasn't the same person, because that would just be weird. What do I sleep with? Usually ibuprofen and a little nip of brandy.

I don't have a problem with sleeping with a teddy bear. It's just that they freak me out, with their little eyes always open; I'm afraid I'll wake up with one hovering over me, holding a cute little teddy knife.

"Would you travel the world with Mark Hunter?" One person answered yes. Clearly, they've never lived with me.

"Is Mark Hunter fun to be around?" Again, one person answered yes, and again, that person has obviously not spent a lot of time around me. I'm a writer. I've heard some working writers are the life of the party, but what I like to do is write, and the actual act of writing is horribly dull to anyone watching it. It's not like music comes out when my fingers dance over the computer keys.

"Do you think MH ever played strip poker?" Trick question. I did indeed once play strip poker, but I bailed as soon as I lost my shirt. In my defense, I was twelve.

"Do you think MH should NOT have children?" This person answered no – which doesn't matter, because that parental ship has sailed.

"Do you think MH can dance?" The answer was no. Good answer.

"Do you think MH can throw a football with a spiral?" The answer was yes. Bad answer. I couldn't launch a football with a cannon.

"Do you think MH could be a gangster?" Two people answered yes. I have no idea where that came from.

One person answered yes to the question of whether I've ever smoked. I have not. Well, once, when I got a little too close to a barn fire, but I don't believe that's what they meant.

Another answered yes, I've gone to a strip club. You'd think that would be correct – I mean, I'm a guy. However, I never have. A strip club, to me, is the equivalent of window shopping: What's the point of going there just to look through the windows, when I can't even touch the merchandise?

Could I shoot someone if I had to? Maybe. Make a sudden turn in front of me without signaling one more time, and you'll find out.

Okay, let's run through a few more quickly:

I have not watched the TV show "24". If I want to see extremists torturing someone, I'll turn on MSNBC. I do *not* recycle dirty underwear, nor do I want to know what that means. I would never ditch a date, having had it happen to me. I have indeed pulled an all-nighter, which I suppose prepared me for my present job. I do like British accents, I did watch *Glee*, and – sorry – I have indeed done things I'm ashamed of.

I don't know what "game" is but, contrary to what was guessed, I don't think I have it.

Some people said I have a nice smile and that I'm cute. I have nothing pithy to say about that, I just wanted to throw it in there.

Sorry, I would not do anything to succeed. If so, I would have succeeded by now.

I'm not cool. Where in the world did you get that? Haven't you even been reading my columns? Yes, I do sometimes sing Britney Spears aloud when no one is around – does that settle the cool question?

Okay, what's a poser, and why does someone think I am one? If it means I'm afraid someone will figure out I have no idea what I'm doing, then they're probably right.

"Do you think MH would ever do community service voluntarily?" This person answered yes, possibly under the assumption that after 30 years as a volunteer firefighter I'm thinking of sticking with it.

"Do you think MH ever watched someone undress secretly?" No, because they kept their curtains closed.

Someone said I don't have a cute butt. Maybe not. How would I know?

Someone else said I don't like chick flicks. Um … I've published two romantic comedy novels. I love romantic comedies. (Dramas, not so much.) My wife likes dude movies: superhero and zombie stuff, things like that. This is the 21st Century, people! Still, is this where the next question came from?

"Do you think MH wants to come out of the closet?"

I'd never go in there in the first place. There are *spiders* in that closet, man! (Someone answered yes to that, by the way.)

And finally:

"Do you think MH is superficial?"

They answered yes to that. *Yes!* Can you believe it?

How could you think I'm superficial, just because I wrote an entire newspaper column that's all about me?

FACTS ARE FACTS, EXCEPT WHEN THEY'RE NOT

I recently stumbled upon a list of amazing facts.

I mean that literally, at least in a literary way: I found the list on a site called "StumbleUpon". You go there and ... stumble upon things, which I did.

Honestly, I don't go there often. I'm not much of a window shopper in real life or on the internet, and when I want to find something on the net I usually search for that specific thing. Granted, I've been known to, after finding that thing, start jumping from link to link and end up spending hours surfing, but at least I start out with a purpose.

Now, I've given you lists of "facts" before. What interested me about these facts involve the comments section, where a group of people called ... um, for our purposes we'll say the commenters called "bullpoop" on the alleged facts. Specifically, they pointed to several items that they said were just plain false.

Hard to believe that could happen on the internet, huh?

For instance, one "fact" was that it's impossible to sneeze with your eyes open. As with many such myths, it was tested by a group of myth busters on the Discovery Channel, who call themselves Mythbusters.

Their conclusion: You *can* sneeze with your eyes open. The only question is, why?

You should usually question it when the facts are followed by an exclamation point. I found this out through years of research! But not having one doesn't mean it's true. Here are some other facts people took issue with:

Adolf Hitler was a vegetarian, and had only one testicle.

"Excuse me, Fuhrer; it's time for your checkup. Drop your pants and cough, please ... holy cow! It just went rolling right out the door! Well, at least you have a spare."

In reality, Hitler's personal physician never mentioned it, and was apparently a conscientious caregiver who would have put it in the records. Unless Hitler told him not to ... 'cause saying no to that guy was probably a dangerous practice.

According to one of Hitler's food tasters – who should know – Adolf followed a vegetarian diet toward the end of his life, but his cook before the war said he was a fan of stuffed pigeon ... which is not a vegetable. I assume. Some refute the idea that he was ever a vegetarian, although I can't help noticing that those who get most voracious in that argument happen to be vegetarians, themselves. One noted vegetarian claims Hitler loved liver dumplings.

Liver dumplings.

Well, we already knew he was evil.

As near as I can tell from more balanced sources, he considered himself a vegetarian after about 1938, but the definition was a bit looser back then (Liver dumplings!). I don't think this reflects on people who don't like meat, any more than eating meat makes you evil. Unless it's liver dumplings.

Here's another "fact": *The population of the world is 5 billion people, and predicted to become 15 billion by 2080!*

What will we feed all these people?! (I suggest liver dumplings.) Especially since the population is closer to 7 billion.

Here's another one: *Your heart beats over 100,000 times a day.* (Oh, excuse me: !)

Um, no. Do the math. Unless my math is wrong. Which has happened.

There's a city called Rome on every continent!

Yeah? Under how much ice is the one on Antarctica buried?

What is called the "French kiss" in the English speaking world is known as an "English kiss" in France!

The French took great exception to this claim. They would name nothing after those uncouth Americans, the French explain. However, when I pressed the issue they surrendered.

Here's my favorite: *It's against the law to have a pet dog in Iceland!*

Well, what dog would want to live in Iceland? They've got ice and volcanos. That's it.

Okay, the truth is that Iceland is greener than Greenland, which is icy. Possibly this is because Iceland is nearer the political capitals of Europe, and thus is bathed in hot air. A more likely story is that the first Vikings to sail west used the name Greenland to attract more settlers. In other words, they lied. The Vikings later established the world's first advertising agency.

But that's not the point, and the claim caused an eruption of icy comments, which often involved name calling of the sort I can't describe here. People took the idea of not having a dog in Iceland *very* seriously, and not just because they were harboring illegal canines.

According to my sources (who are all on the internet, so there you go), it was once against the law to have a pet dog in one city in Iceland. This was because in Reykjavik people were too busy learning how to spell the name of their city to take care of a dog. The laws are still strict on dog ownership there, but it's not illegal.

So there you go. If all those claims are false, how can I believe the other claims? Maybe slugs don't have four noses. Maybe dolphins don't sleep with one eye open. Maybe everyone's tongue print isn't different. Maybe wasps don't taste like pine nuts.

Who tastes wasps, anyway?

Besides, what do pine nuts taste like? Other than wasps?

Someday, I'll stumble upon the answer.

TALKING BACK TO SPAM

Remember awhile back when I wrote a column about spam e-mails? *(Don't bother looking— that column's not in this book. You'll just have to take my word for it.)* Well, I've found myself actually talking back to spam lately.

I don't mean the food product in the store; I mean, I've talked to food in the store before, but usually only to say "I'm on a diet! Leave me alone!" I'm talking about junk mail in the comfort of my own home, where I can safely talk out loud without being hauled away, though the dog does silently mock me. These unread spam messages pop up in my e-mail's junk mailbox, I check to make sure it's nothing important, and the next thing you know I'm talking back to some idiot in Bangladesh who sent the exact same message to three billion other people.

At first I did it because I got mad, but these days it's kind of fun. After all, junk mail is no more dangerous than your eighty-third credit card offer in regular mail. Why waste ill temper on them when there are computer virus makers to hate, instead?

So I have a little fun with the subject and "from" lines:

"Dearest in the Lord" ...

Well, Kittitach Pichatwatana – can I call you Kittitach? I hope so, because I strained my tongue pronouncing your last name. Well, Kittitach, it's nice of you to write from all the way in Uttar Pradesh to let me know I'm dearest in the Lord, but that strikes me as just a bit egotistical.

On a name related note, I got an e-mail with nothing on the subject line from someone called DarkEmber Dreamgirl. While it's possible that's her World of Warcraft elf name, I think it's more likely she wanted to invite me into, shall we say, the seamy underbelly of the internet.

"NAME BRAND TIRE DISCOUNTS!"

Online, typing something in all caps means you're yelling. Dude, don't yell at me. Since I was a kid, I haven't reacted well to yelling. Send me the tires, then we'll talk.

"Reduced cruise packages available."

But I don't *want* to go on a reduced cruise. If I'm going on a cruise, I want a regular sized ship.

"Search local singles in your area at Match.com!"

My wife won't let me. Besides, if I was going to search for singles they wouldn't be in my area; e-mailing someone who lives across the street seems pointless. Ahem – not that I haven't done it.

"Your quick reply needed ..."

Too late. Should have been quicker.

"Half off at top local restaurants!"

Top half? Bottom half? Either way, somebody's sure to call the police.

"$47.99 Egyptian cotton Duvet covers."

I don't even know what a Duvet is. Maybe a compact car manufactured in Egypt? Do you cover it to protect the finish, or so the neighbors won't laugh at you? Besides, what's wrong with American cotton? Although I suppose they could just ship the cover over in the Duvet's trunk.

"Guaranteed credit card approvals! Find your card."

Okay, I found it. Now what? Look, the problem with "guaranteed" approval is that if it's guaranteed, it's probably not worth the paperwork or the stamp to send it in. It reminds me of the old Groucho Marx line about not joining any club that would have me as a member.

"Dear beloved one:"

How nice, but I've never met you. Are you a friend of Kittitach Pichatwatana?

"View black singles in your city!"

Okay, that strikes me as *just* a bit racist. What would the reaction be if an invitation read, "View white singles in your city!"? Oh, wait – that was the next junk mail.

"Your exclusive Invitation to join!"

Yeah, me and several hundred million other people. Join what, anyway? The sender is listed as being "Beyond The Rack", which would mean anything from custom tailored suits to the backroom at a San Francisco sex dungeon. Or both, and wouldn't that be a great way to diversify your business?

"Hello."

Um ... hello, Wenzhou Ourvis. How do you react to a subject line like that? You click on it, and next thing you know the computer's being taken over by an internet poltergeist with Arnold Schwarzenegger's voice. (Just for fun, I'm going to leave Arnold's last name just as I spelled it, without checking. We'll see how I did.) But at the same time, you have to feel a little sorry for the poor guy whose parents named him Wenzhou.

"Pay your house off in 5-7 years!"

Well, yay! That'll be great, as long as I don't have to refinance to pay for a roof replacement ... oh, darn.

"READ AND GET BACK TO ME."

Make me. I told you not to yell.

"I WANT YOU TO BE MY BUSINESS PARTNER."

I want you to stop yelling. Sometimes I think the biggest maintenance problem with keyboards is when the caps lock sticks in the on position. Although, in all fairness, maybe Hakem Hani has to yell to get through the bad connection from Ulan Bator.

"Earn a degree while you earn a living!"

Those University of Phoenix people want me, bad. Let me just clear any sleep periods off my schedule, and I'll sign right up.

And here's my favorite:

"Attn: MoneyGram alert."

That seems a bit tempting; I actually am expecting money from someone oversees, after all. However, a closer look reveals that 18,000,000 pounds (at today's exchange rate, that's roughly three thousand ObamaBucks) is awaiting me, while what I'm actually expecting is less than twenty dollars for a copy of my book.

Hyperinflation is as bad as caps lock shouting, in the junk mail world.

MR. JOHNSON HUNG UP ON ME

At work the other day we received a very nice fax, from Mrs. Nazek Audi Hariri. I'm sure you've heard of her husband, Rafik Baha al-din Hariri. Or at least, it's possible you once raised a din while driving your Audi in Baha.

Mrs. Audi Hariri offered to give us 20% of 36 million dollars.

I thought to myself, Well, we're all getting raises *this* year!

It seems her husband, a respected businessman and politician in Lebanon, was killed in an explosion on Valentine's Day, 2005. Tragic, right? But afterward, Mrs. Hariri was contacted by a European security firm, which held a trunk that belonged to her husband – a trunk containing the aforementioned three dozen million bucks, all in cash, which no doubt cushioned the lady's grief and provided a nice little late Valentine gift.

Apparently the money was from business associates, and was meant to be used for Mr. Hariri's next election campaign. I'm guessing the campaign finance laws work a little differently in Lebanon.

This is all good, what with her giving us 20%, which amounts to, um, let me do some quick math ... $76,000,000. I'm guessing I forgot to carry a decimal point, there. (Hey, I'm not used to dealing with any number over three digits.) Let's try again ... okay, now I've got it at 7 mil, give or take. And really, at that point do a few hundred more bucks really matter? I could buy a lot of ramen with a seven and six ones.

Now, here's where things get a bit fuzzy: The reason Mrs. Hairy sent this fax is because a person receiving it, identified by her as "you", is one of her husband's business partners. But the fax came to my work, and anybody working there who had enough money to contribute toward a multi-million dollar campaign fund would NOT be working there.

Mrs. Heshe explained it all in this clear and concise sentence:

"The part of services the diplomat is required to render is to assist you in claiming the consignments from the terminal of the security company and to set up a transit domiciliary account in your name in one of the prime bank he has contacts to carry out the exercise through the back door."

Oh. Well, when you put it that way, it all makes sense: She's sending her money through the back door.

Besides, I checked into the story. There really was a Lebanese Prime Minister Rafik Hariri, who really was killed in an explosion, and he really was estimated to be worth billions. Which is like millions, only more. He even has a son named Baha:

"What are you going to name your son?"

"Baha."

"Well, what happens in California stays in California. Where are you vacationing next year?"

"Saadeddine."

"Oh boy."

Granted, I wasn't able to find much mention of Mrs. Hibijibi. But I got everything else off the internet, so it must be true.

I immediately called her contact person, a diplomat in London named Mark Johnson. "I'd like to help with the Audi Hariri Funny Honey Money Fund," I told him.

"You would?" I couldn't figure out why he was so surprised. After all, 20% of 36 million is ... um ... well, so much money that I'll never have to do math again.

"I sure do. I mean, the poor lady's so oppressed that she can't even go through her front door! If this keeps up, they'll take her names away, one by one. First she won't have an Audi, then she won't be Hariri any more, and next thing you know she'll never get to go to Baha again."

"Ah, yes ..." He seemed a little uncertain about whether I was for real, which I can understand – after all, people do crazy things for that much money. "Well, with this much cash flow involved, you must understand that certain guarantees will be needed, certain, ah, capital assistance to provide for the transference of funds."

"Well," I said, "I live in the capital of Noble County. Does that help?"

"What I'm saying is, a certain amount of financial incentive on your part will be needed to assist in the transference of cash into your account."

"Are you saying I need to send you money in order to get money? So in return for services, you need a financial contribution?"

"Well ... yes."

"So you're like the federal government?"

"Um –"

I thought about that for a moment. "Look, here's the thing. Mrs. Hihickey obviously needs our help, so how about if you bring the money over yourself? It just so happens that we have a place, right in the building where I work, where you can stay while we get this all sorted out. You'll get a nice bed, three square meals a day, entertainment, and even people who'll stay with you and help you acclimate into our society."

"Really? Where would that be?"

"The Noble County Jail. Now, if you'll just give me your –"

But that's when Mr. Mark Johnson hung up, and he wouldn't answer my return calls. Honestly, I'm beginning to suspect he wasn't on the level.

INTERSTITIAL POEM, INCOMPLETE

T'was the month before winter, and I have to admit

I'd gone on a bender, just thinking of it.

All the usual symptoms of winter depression

made it clear that cruel season would soon be in session.

My fav girl and I had just settled down,

though no cap was involved, and surely no gown.

We planned to sleep in, and not leave the joint;

with wind and rain pounding what would be the point?

Then came a slight cough, and a little throat clearing.

a sniffle announced that our world was veering

into a bad place, the place that I hate –

which began when she said "I don't feel so great."

WHY MY WIFE IS AWESOME

There are ways in which my wife and I are very different. For instance, she's female. (I'm a guy. These days you need to specify.) She's half my age, which some people find more disturbing than the question of gender. She's from the south, and I'm from a place people from the south used to migrate to. She's smart, and I'm a smart aleck.

Now, there are also a lot of things we have in common, mostly geek type stuff and a mutual hatred of winter. But I can tell you why I'm attracted to my wife in one simple statement:

She has a sword collection.

How awesome is that?

Oh, sure, she won't let me touch any of them. She feels very strongly that I already have enough scars. But still, she has one (a collection, not a scar), and you don't get much cooler than a bundle of blades just waiting to go up against ninjas or a zombie horde.

I do have my own collection: a pirate sword, a saber, and a lightsaber. All plastic. But that's fine, because when I get a bladed weapon I tend to swing it around, and then hit either furniture or myself. We can't afford to replace the furniture, and I can only imagine the price tag for reattaching a foot.

There's a certain irony that we had to get a gun and a big dog to keep anyone from stealing the sword collection, but irony runs strong in my household.

It all started when I was searching around to get Emily a gift. If there was ever an example of a person you shouldn't make gender assumptions about, it's her. I played with more dolls as a kid than she did. (Ahem. Action figures. G.I. Joe, Johnny West—don't make me get defensive.) I knew her well enough that my first impulse was, of course, to get her a lightsaber.

Turns out they don't make those things for real. I suspect it's for the best.

So instead, I got her a full tang battle ready Katana. (That's a sword.) I handed it to her, and it was Christmas! That's not an expression, it was literally Christmas. Let me tell you, getting the tree hauled outside wasn't a problem that year.

We also have a saber, which was actually given to me by a friend, but I'm not allowed anything that isn't small and dull enough to butter bread. Ever try to butter bread with a saber? Makes a mess, although not as much as an arterial bleed.

Then, at a garage sale, we found another katana. I don't know what the plural of that is; if I saw someone carrying a katana in each hand, I wouldn't be inclined to ask. Finally, my father-in-law gave her a friggin' Marine sword. What message he was trying to send me I don't know, but you can't pass by a real U.S. Marine sword without standing just a bit straighter.

You can't help but love a woman with a sword collection. She said she might even let me practice with one someday, once she's double checked the insurance policy. I'm sure she can handle a zombie apocalypse by herself, but she might need help with a ninja invasion.

Nobody puts Emi in a corner. Well, sometimes she does.

PART THREE:

medical stuff, and things

I laugh at patient confidentiality forms. I laugh because, whenever I have a major medical problem, I immediately start thinking about the column potentials.

No incident is too embarrassing. Colonoscopy? Something to shove into the newspaper. Diverticulitis? Let's dive right into the discussion. Once, while mowing my lawn, I beaned myself on a tree branch and quite literally went head over heels. If someone had been filming it, I'd have hit a YouTube record that would have embarrassed Miley Cyrus ... and she's doesn't embarrass easily. Writing about it would make me seem ridiculous. It would also make deadline, so I did.

Medical stuff is number three on the list of my most often written about things. That list, by the way, is:

1. Writing. (Yes, I recognize the irony.)
2. Home maintenance fails. (Home maintenance success isn't funny, or so I assume.)
3. Medical stuff. (The older I get, the more that subject comes up.)

4. Stupid things from the internet. (Since I tend to hold that stuff back for a rainy day, you're getting a lot of it now.)
5. Holidays. (If you can't find something funny about dressing weird and eating stuff you'd normally avoid, you should get your Humor Club card revoked.)
6. Firefighting. (This is something I have to be careful with. Like most people in the emergency services, firefighters tend to have a dark sense of humor that doesn't always translate.)
7. Stupid things I *learned* from the internet—which I'll grant you is close to #4. (Because, after all, the human race has always reveled in the silly.)
8. Family. (Not as much as before, because the family has begun to figure out where I hide.)
9. Politics. (In addition to not enjoying the knee-jerk reaction of one-third of the readers, I've learned as I get older that stupid stuff in politics has deadly serious consequences.)
10. Parenthesis. (I overdo them. I don't know why, but maybe someday I'll get it under control.)
    (Or maybe not.)
    (ed: definitely not.)

OPEN WIDE AND SAY "OW"

I wanted to throw this in as an example of just how shameless I can be at promoting my books. Now, when you finish this, go buy my other books.

I'm having a colonoscopy tomorrow, and it gave me an idea for how to increase sales of my novel and short story collection.

Now, hear me out.

As all fourteen of my regular readers know, I have a newspaper column (*Well, I DID ...*), and often use my personal experiences as material to fill those 52 pieces a year. But the question is, does anyone want to hear yet another description of one of the most disturbing medical procedures a male ever goes through?

I think not.

After all, Dave Barry has already written the ultimate humor column on the subject, while comedian Jeff Foxworthy did a screamingly funny routine along the same lines. All I could do is cover the same ground and leave my readers possibly smiling, but almost certainly uncomfortable.

That's when it came to me: Blackmail.

That's right, people. If I don't sell ... I don't know ... ten copies of *Storm Chaser* and/or *Storm Chaser Shorts* between now and the end of the month, I *will* write a column about my colonoscopy. I'll hide the subject matter, so you'll be three paragraphs in before you realize what you're reading, and by then it'll be too late. Yep.

But if sales pick up – if you call your sisters and cousins and aunts, and beg them, for the love of all that's holy, to buy something from me before it's too late – then you'll be safe. No routines about the "prep". No fire hose jokes. No comparisons to the space shuttle launching. Not even one mention of "probing Uranus".

I'm drinking the prep stuff as we talk, people: There's no time to waste. Go to **MarkRHunter.com**, or look me up at **WhiskeyCreekPress.com**, **Amazon.com/Mark-R-Hunter/e/B0058CL6OO,** or **BarnesandNoble.com/c/Mark-R-Hunter**.

Do it for your own comfort. To stop the nightmares. Do it because my health savings account just ran dry. Do it for humanity.

SEMI-COLON: YOU DIDN'T DO IT

Sales didn't pick up that week—that week mentioned above when my below got probed. Any future uncomfortable medical discussions will be the fault of you who didn't buy my books.

You know who you are. It's on your hands.

Not literally ... ick.

PUTTING THE FINGER ON
PROSTATE SCREENING

Prostate. Another of those words that strike fear into the hearts of men, much like the terms "cholesterol", "mother-in-law", and "where are we going with this relationship?"

Not my mother-in-law—I like my mother-in-law. Don't judge me as a humorist. Besides, she's probably reading this.

You might say I arrived at my prostate problem through the back door ...

You know there's no way to deal with this without a little inappropriate wordplay, right?

I never thought much about my prostate, because the men in my family die of heart attacks. There are exceptions, but I never gave it much thought until approaching that age myself.

That made me think: "Hey, I don't wanna die". Look, I don't pretend to know what Heaven's like, but you can be darn sure there's no chocolate in Hell. Why take the chance?

Add to that the fact that I married a woman half my age, and now I have to keep up with her. This led to increased attention to my health, which led to a routine blood test, which led to a high PSA reading. A lot of Prostate Specific Antigens can mean something's wrong ... or not. Experts now believe false positives might lead to unneeded biopsies and high patient anxiety.

I can attest to both.

A routine blood screening is how I got into this position to begin with, and boy, is that position embarrassing. Especially with a female doctor, because the next step was the Test That Must Not Be Named, the one that strikes fear into the heart of all men. Well, maybe the fear is a bit lower than the heart. Let's just say that in an electronic age, this test is digital.

What would be better for the test, a male or female physician? A male doctor can understand where you're coming from while he's going in. On the other hand, straight men aren't necessarily thrilled by having another guy come at them from that position, not to mention the woman's fingers are generally smaller.

By the way: You can make all the jokes you want, but sexual orientation means nothing here. I'll guarantee you gay men don't like that procedure under those circumstances any more than straight men do. It's not like they're getting a candlelit dinner and a bow-wrapped CD of Judy Garland hits. And why didn't my wife get me that as a reward for going in the first place?

As my problem turned out to be long-term, I got a chance to go both ways. Okay, let me rephrase: I got examined by both male and female doctors. I even took my wife along to one checkup; she's a sport.

"Hm," the doctor said during the procedure. "You have a spongy apex."

"Oh," my wife said, "You're a psychiatrist, too?"

Do I really have to talk, during a moment when the doc's searching for my appendix and I'm in a position normally only seen on reruns of *Cops*? "I think that's my tonsil, doc. Say, does this mean we're in a relationship?"

"Might as well be – I think I lost my wedding ring up there."

"Don't worry; it'll all come out in the end."

It's nice to have a doctor with a sense of humor. I elected not to shake her hand afterward, though.

To make a long finger short, we decided to watch the situation (not literally – ew). What followed was a series of PSA tests and, yes, high patient anxiety. Yeah, let's just start the next few months with "you might have cancer ... maybe not. Maybe. Have a nice winter, see you next quarter."

PSA tests remain controversial. I suspect many doctors continue them because they're a simple blood test, as opposed to another simple procedure that alien abductees are all too familiar with. Maybe Earth is simply a testing ground for little green urologists?

I don't care how much money you make as a doctor, no way can you be all that thrilled about greasing up your fingers and getting to know your patient's better half. If you are, maybe you belong in a different industry, one concentrated in basement dungeons on the West Coast.

Still, a series of high PSA counts is a pattern, which led me to the next step in my long, hard path: A biopsy. I learned many things during this process. I wish I hadn't.

At least my urologist would do the procedure: A male, who would understand the discomfort factor. Best of all, his office was in Fort Wayne, which meant I didn't know his family and friends, and wasn't likely to meet him on the street.

Silly me. Specialists don't do those kinds of "procedures".

No, mine was done by a very nice lady who I learned, during the small talk that makes me want to ask for general anesthesia, is the sister of the woman who cuts my hair. That sister is married to a guy I work with.

I had to not only find a different barber, but I'm searching for a different home in a different state.

The biopsy wasn't all that painful, but in no way can somebody make it comfortable. That opening's designed for one way traffic, people. While the biopsy needle itself is tiny, the device it's attached to is roughly the size and shape of a jack hammer, and makes a similar noise each time a sample is taken.

Not one sample. Dozens and dozens of samples, to the point where I wanted to ask, "Why not just take out the whole thing now?"

Instead, being a person who makes jokes in uncomfortable situations, I said all those things she's heard thousands of times:

"Hey, you're tickling my ribs."

"Ever tried haggis?"

"I understand not getting flowers, but you could have bought me dinner. But no haggis."

"Do you think they'll ever name a planet *My*anus?"

Finally they gave me a prescription for antibiotics and sent me on my way, with the warning that I might experience "some" discomfort. I didn't anticipate the discomfort striking as I waited at the pharmacy. Next time someone offers to drive me to a doctor's appointment I'm going to say yes, even if I don't want anyone to know where I'm going.

And after all that, what were the results?

Exactly the same as back when I got my first PSA reading. "You might have cancer ... maybe not. Maybe. Have a nice summer, see you next quarter."

Three years later my PSA rates haven't gone up, haven't gone down, and haven't given me decent lottery numbers. The good news is, if I have to get another biopsy it won't seem like such a big deal. Why? Because I just hit 50 ...

And it's time for my colonoscopy.

*You wrote a column about **what**?*

UTERUS VS. UROLOGIST:
BRINGING COUPLES TOGETHER
THROUGH MEDICAL TESTING
OR:
DON'T DO IT

BY EMILY HUNTER

(Mark's note: I figured on this subject, we should get an opinion from the other end.)

You know what's worse than getting a prostate exam?

Watching someone get a prostate exam.

I knew when I started dating a guy significantly older than me I'd have to deal with certain things health-wise. I accepted the injuries from his years on the local volunteer fire department (and the potential for many more) because the selflessness behind them made him the kind of guy I'd like to marry. In his mid-forties, though, I never expected the Prostate Inquisition.

No one ever does.

Now guys, as awful and embarrassing and awkward as you think getting your prostate poked is ... well, it looks even weirder while you're watching it being done to your fiancé. *(Mark's note: But she still married me!)* I still suspect he only married me so I'd keep my mouth shut, or maybe because I passed some sort of extreme rite-of-passage test.

I didn't think they'd do it in front of me. I was just there to remember the stuff he'd forget in five seconds, make sure he followed the doctor's orders, and be Moral Support.

There is obviously a fine line between moral support and *Oh good gravy get me the hell out of here*. Neither us can find that line on a map.

Two years later, he realized what I meant by, "You think that's bad? Try getting a mammogram! Wait 'till you see a pap smear and exam!" when I began to have Girl Parts Problems.

But that was later, before he had the biopsy. When he had it, I was 500 miles away doing the whole college-education business, so unfortunately I couldn't be a pain in the ass to him while he had a pain in his ass. Or help him inflate his little donut thing.

But he was right there for all of my procedures. Waiting while I was in surgery. Making tea. Fluffing pillows. Helping me to the bathroom. Desperately trying to convince a seriously medicated me that my entrails could not possibly come out of the stitched-up incision in my bellybutton.

We ended up going through the Months of a Thousand Tests again, only with the opposite parts. Nobody could figure out what was wrong to explain my horrible pain, and my intense hormone levels got even worse while I worried about what was happening to me during my rounds of testing. I was on antibiotics over Valentine's Day. I was too sick to enjoy to our 'this-is-just-our-legal-marriage' wedding night. I cried during sad puppy commercials, sappy moments on comedy shows, inspirational movie trailers, and once during River Monsters, a show about giant fish.

My laparoscopy showed that I have endometriosis. They patched up a few things while they were in there, and I'll be on medication for a long time. It's not great news, but I get to keep my Girl Parts, and the regular check-ups won't be so bad. That, and, according to my RN from my brief stay, I have to return to the hospital weekly to fulfill the donut clause in the forms I signed. Real donuts for the RN, not the ones my hubby sits on.

For now, we'll both be taking all kinds of preventative and treatment meds, kicking up the exercise, and eating healthier. Maybe we can get a couple's version of those monthly pill boxes with the little date windows.

They found out what's wrong with my junk, but not his – just because his biopsy came back clean doesn't mean there's not some tiny cancerous cell hiding in the abyss down there, biding its time like an evil dictator with something to prove. Still, no "big C" news is good news. Besides, prostate cancer is slow moving, anyway, and he runs into burning buildings on a regular basis. (Of course, he's relatively safe there; the real danger is when he tries to do home repairs.) It's not that I'm not worried – it's just that, having married an accident-prone hero, my worry has to be hierarchal.

So, he gets regular checkups. And we Wait. And we Monitor. And we make horrible butt jokes.

I'm staying in the damn waiting room during his colonoscopy.

(Mark's notes: Hey! ... no, that's all pretty accurate.)

BELLY ACHING IS MY LIFE

The subject I'm writing about today is very painful for me.

I mean, physically painful.

I think maybe there was subconscious jealousy of my wife, who's fighting a medical ailment that has one of those long, scary sounding names. Out loud I might have said, "I'm sorry you're hurting, dear, but on the brighter side I'm feeling fine."

(I wouldn't have said that, mind you – I'm not stupid.)

But subconsciously, maybe I was thinking, "Hey—you can't beat me on this illness thing. I deserve my shot at sympathy!" Apparently the chronic back pain, tennis elbow, and shoulder problem weren't enough: I needed something that would take me at least four syllables to describe.

On a side note, at what point in the human race did we take pride in having a physical problem worse than the guy we're talking to?

"My prostate's the size of a softball. I haven't peed in three years."

"Oh, yeah? My prostate's so big it has satellite prostates orbiting around it. I never know for sure whether I've got hemorrhoids or asteroids."

But I digress because … well, because I don't want to talk about it. But by gosh, I'm going to make *some* money off this thing, in addition to grabbing my pity rights back from a woman whose only problems were intense, debilitating pain, unrelated pharyngitis, and putting up with me.

So I developed a belly ache.

It's another irony of humanity that many of us brag incessantly about our physical ailments, while the others ignore them in the theory they'll pout and go away. Some of us somehow manage to do both at the same time, by whining and complaining while not actually taking action to solve the problem. This last talent is perfected by, ironically, both the Washington politician and the non-voting citizen.

Eventually the pain, in the lower left quadrant of my abdomen, got bad enough that I progressed from the ignoring stage to the whining stage. This is marked by drawing my words out while speaking in a high voice: "Myyyy stooomach huuuuurrrrrttttsssss..."

"So," Emily replied, "call the doctor."

"I don't waaaaannnnnaaaaaa....."

When I finally did call the doctor, it was with the expectation that they would pat me on the back, give me a lollypop, and send me home with a bottle of something pink and awful tasting. I mean, it was a belly ache, in the dull and unimportant left lower quadrant. It didn't even hurt *that* much. That is, until they pushed on it.

They prodded, took a pint of every bodily fluid, did some other things I'd rather not discuss. By the way, I don't think my doctor likes me anymore: Every time we meet, he gives me the finger.

The blood and urine tests pronounced me normal. The psychological testing gave them pause.

The diagnosis: Diverticulitis. I quickly counted up the syllables: seven! That's one more than Emily's endometriosis. I win! Only after I realize I'd miscounted, and we were in fact tied, did I pause to think: "Am I going to die? And if so, could they find something with one more syllable? Like ... DieDiverticulitus?"

Not to get too technical, but diverticulitis is a condition in which an inflamed area cuts the colon's operation in half, leaving it a semicolon, which isn't really true but is an old punctuation joke dear to my writing heart. Researchers speculate it can be caused by a lack of fiber, which is ridiculous because there's fiber in fruit, and fruit flavor goes into Mountain Dew, so there.

To rest and settle my intestines while the antibiotics went to work, the doctor put me on the BRAT diet. I thought, hey, great: I *love* brats! Turns out I had the pronunciation wrong, and BRAT in fact stands for bananas, rice, apples, and toast. I like all of those things (although I sneaked butter into half of them), so it took me awhile to realize it's not really all that healthy in the long term. Still, thanks to Emily's cooking magic I actually ate better than I would have on my own, and my belly didn't hurt except for the one time I tried to substitute BRAT with brat.

So, all's well that ends well ... except, speaking of ends, the doctor only *suspected* I had diverticulitis. It could be anything from an ulcer, to cancer, to all that gum I swallowed as a child working its way through. For further diagnosis, he gave me the choice of barium enema or colonoscopy.

Some choice.

But it wasn't a choice for two reasons: First, I turn fifty this year, and my beloved had already told me in no uncertain terms that a man with my smoking history (I never smoked, but a lot of the buildings I ran into as a firefighter did), needed that routine test.

Second, colonoscopy sounds like a procedure, while barium enema sounds like the title of a cable TV sitcom episode.

Here's the best part: I'm going to have my colposcopy done during my already scheduled vacation. That was *not* on the itinerary.

But it's been the year for such things. Seems like all my columns this year have been about writing or medical stuff, and although the medical columns were probably funnier, I'd as soon go the other way. No editor ever tried to give me a prostate exam.

Although sometimes it seemed like it.

I FORGOT WHAT THIS ONE IS ABOUT

There's this internet trivia game where you have to answer trivia questions ... on the internet.

Yeah, I guess that's pretty self-explanatory.

I don't play it myself, because of my addictive nature. Last time I tried to play a video game regularly they had to do an intervention before I starved to death. Still, I get asked trivia questions by other people who play it, especially questions about history. How, they wonder, do I know so much? I know, for instance, which President got stuck in a bathtub, which two Presidents died on the same July 4th, and who is buried in Grant's tomb. Okay, that last one's not so hard, but still ... everyone should know Mrs. Grant is in there.

And that's it. I can remember nothing else. Not what I just had for dinner, not where I put my glasses, not if the dog's out or in, not if the dog is wearing my glasses and eating my dinner, nothing. There's only so much room in there, you see. In my brain, not the dog.

I'm especially notorious for not remembering names and faces. Being a bit introverted, I'm loathe to wave at someone if I'm not absolutely sure I know them. There's no doubt I've lost friends and un-influenced people because of this. Worse, I also don't

71

remember who's driving what car, so if someone drives by me and waves they could be a friend, or someone being attacked by a bee.

This causes many embarrassing situations. The worst is when I do book signings, because I'll see people I've known for decades, and have absolutely no idea what their name is ... and I have to write their names. My wife helps if she's already met the people, because she has a good memory for names ... or maybe just better than mine. I can't remember. Emily's like that guy who stands by the President at White House gatherings, whispering the identity and associations of people coming down the reception line:

"That's Marcia, sir, her architect father helped design your new White House caddy shack."

"Marcia! How's Jan? Oh, she tried to kill you and is in prison again? Well, somebody should have given her a Snickers, you know how grouchy she gets when her blood sugar is low. Middle kids, huh?"

(Here's an irony: A few months before I wrote this, a commercial came out that had *Marsha* eating a Snickers.)

Sadly, I can't afford to fill that position, and Emily isn't originally from around here, so she can be of only so much help. "Do you recognize that guy?" I'll ask.

"Hey," she'll reply, "It's *your* family reunion."

But I can't help it. When I do remember names, I can't place them with faces. When I recognize faces, I can't tell from where. Did I once work with them? Did we wrestle over the last donut at a training function? Are they one of my kids?

"Excuse me, did my ex-wife give birth to you?"

"I honestly don't remember, Dad ..."

The worst time this ever happened to me was once when I was talking to a lady, and she suddenly realized I didn't recognize her. I mean, we all have our faults—she didn't need to be so offended. She went all overboard and started yelling, "But Mark ... I'm your *mother*."

Hey, it wasn't my fault she changed her hair style.

I'm told this is what my office looks like without clutter.
They were filming me for ... something.

PART FOUR:

The writer's life for me
or:
brother, can you spare a dime?

Why do writers write?

For profit? If you haven't heard me complaining about money by now, you're not one of my fourteen regular readers. For fame? For every Stephen King there's an obscure writer named Norman Kowalski. Norman has been working on the same all-American novel for eighteen years, three wives, and one AA program.

Or Agnes Rudding, who self-published her novel about the 1745 Croatian Revolution, and to this day doesn't know she got the date completely wrong ... and the location. No one noticed, because she sold less than fifty copies of that book. In fact, she's self-published sixty-two novels, and none have sold more than fifty copies. In desperation, she titled her last book James Patterson's Harry Potter's Twilight Outlander.

Or Marilyn Ardor, who actually has gained success, with twenty romance novels published in the last seventeen years. She has two mortgages, drives a twenty year old car, and has missed every one of her children's school functions because of her fourteen hour days. Marilyn, whose real name is Agnes Kowalski (no relation), can't afford to stop being successful.

No, writers write because they have to. You have to breathe, we have to write. Well, we have to breathe, too. Let's not get silly.

HARRY POTTER AND THE CUCKOO'S CALLING

We should all have the problems of J.K. Rowling.

Rowling, or Jo, as I call her when we have tea together, is so famous and insanely popular that she had to publish a novel under a fake name just to see if people would still like her writing.

Poor Jo.

Rowling became Robert Galbraith, a retired member of the British military and father of two sons (named, I suspect, Harry and Ron). He apparently got bored in retirement or couldn't pay the bills on his pension, and so decided to pen a detective story called *The Cuckoo's Calling*.

Ah, but the book's protagonist wasn't the only detective. An intrepid reporter discovered Galbraith shared an editor and agent with the aforementioned J.K.

Apparently it was a slow news day, because the reporter sent the book to two linguistic analysts, who compared it to Rowling's other work. I'd have to guess that other work includes the adventures of a certain young wizard.

Rowling's previous post-Potter book earned mixed reviews, so maybe Rowling got a little paranoid about her talent. The best way to tell if people loved her for her ability or her fame: Hide the fame.

Here's the fun part: As written by Galbraith, the story of the Cuckoo and its call got rave reviews. Mischief managed, and put me down as one who wants to read the new book.

What everyone has forgotten is that it wasn't Rowling's first time at this. Joanne became J.K. to hide her gender – after all, what young boy would want to read the adventures of another young boy as penned by a woman?

I'd like to have seen the experiment go on for a while longer. Better yet, I want to take part, preferably by being a rich and famous author with nothing to prove. Barring that, this whole thing has left me musing over the subject of pseudonyms.

I prefer the term pennames, because it's way easier to spell. Some authors use pennames because they're so prolific that under one name they'd flood the market, which is why Stephen King became Richard Bachman. King's son used a penname to get out from under his dad's considerable shadow. Others switch genres, and don't want their young adult readers to know about their series of hot and spicy romances.

Some switch genders instead of genres, and that may very well be where I'll come in.

This has been going on for decades. Women have published in what was once a male dominated science fiction market, often using initials as Rowling did: D.C. Fontana was one of my favorites, from work on novels and TV shows like *Star Trek*.

In the romance genre it's the exact opposite: In an area dominated by female readers, it was assumed they wanted a female writer. When I decided to write romance I dove into reading as many of them as I could, and one of my favorite authors was Andrea Edward, who hailed from the Michiana area. Only later did I discover Andrea Edwards was Ed and Anne Kolaczk. In addition to the gender question, you can see how spelling that last name might be a problem.

Were the two, a man and woman romance writing team, successful? Well, they published over sixty novels under six names (all female), so ...

When Whiskey Creek Press bought my first romantic comedy, I assumed I'd have to change my gender. (I don't mean literally – let's not go overboard.) To what? Mary Hunter? Hunny Marcus? I suggested to my wife that I use our middle names and become Jane Richards, but it doesn't really sing.

But times have changed, and to my surprise WCP published me under my real name. While everyone who's read my first book liked it (so far as I know), I couldn't say how many refused to pick it up because of my sex. Personally, I think it was a gutsy move on the part of my publisher.

But times haven't changed *that* much.

Not long ago I sent a query letter and sample chapters of a new novel to the largest publisher of romances, Harlequin. A bit to my surprise, an editor there liked it and asked for the full manuscript. Now, that's not an acceptance: I don't know how many full manuscript requests lead to publication (and not for lack of trying to find out), but it's far from all of them.

However, it did get me thinking about that penname thing again. Harlequin does have male authors, and male/female author teams; but you won't see that on their covers. A small price to pay for a foot into that publishing door.

But what penname would I pick?

I'm thinking of becoming: J.K. Rowling.

I mean, it sounds like a writer, doesn't it? And it's perfectly legal, as long as I don't actually claim to be *that* J.K. Rowling. Let's face it, it's not the first really bad idea I've ever had.

This time next year, you might be fooled into thinking the bad ideas are coming from someone else.

RADIO KILLED THE LITERARY STAR

This is my third summer in a row spending way too much time doing publicity for a new book, otherwise known as telling people how great I am. My momma would have beaten me for bragging like that. She might, yet.

The summertime thing is a coincidence – maybe I can swing it to be winter next time, so I can spend more summer days outside, being eaten by insects like normal people.

What have I learned? That I can survive, for one thing. That's not to say I'll ever like it much – I'd rather be writing, and writing's not a spectator sport. Just the same, every now and then a writer gets the attention of the local media, and when that happens you need to do or say something photogenic. How does a writer get the attention of people with cameras?

Be a male who writes a romance novel.

Be a male who wrote a romance novel and later produces a book about local history.

Sell your book to a movie production company for a whole bunch of money.

Two out of three ain't bad.

How do you *not* attract the attention of the media?

Publish a collection of short stories on e-book only.

Really screw up TV and radio interviews. Actually, that could get you the wrong kind of attention, the viral YouTube kind.

The last one worried me. I'd been on TV before, back in 2011, so at least I knew what to expect. But now I'd also be on the radio, and there's one big problem with that: It's live. The TV reporter could edit out my screw-ups and make me look good.

Newspaper interviews were no problem at all, because hey – it's writing. I may be hopeless in most areas, but I know writing.

Anyway, since just about everyone could get their fifteen minutes of fame, I thought I'd pass on some of the advice learned from my exposure to being exposed. To say I'm no expert is putting it mildly, but that's never stopped me before.

TV's the Holy Grail for writers who want to get their names out there, but it's also a trap. Writers – and there are exceptions – are often not all that photogenic. Many of us are also not good speakers – that's the whole reason I started writing – but again, that can be edited.

But when you spend eight hours a day at a desk or sitting on the couch with your laptop, you look like you've spent eight hours a day at a desk. If you've got a sedentary full time job and write on the side, you're going to look like you've spent sixteen hours a day at a desk. Imagine what a vampire would look like if he only drank the blood of very obese people. Pale, spreading out, maybe with a perpetual scowl from rejection letters, and that sunk-eyed look from staring at computer screens. Like a computer gamer, only without having as much fun.

Rule one: Exercise, people. Go see the sun, too.

Don't keep glancing at the camera. I caught myself doing that a couple of times, but try to avoid it. It makes you look like someone who's just been caught by "America's Most Wanted".

Get pictures taken of you beforehand and study them to see your best and worst features. Not long before my interview, I shaved my beard off. Only then did I realize why people liked my beard: It covered my chin.

Practice. Many writers have not voluntarily spoken in public for years. You know who you are. Get some practice in beforehand.

If the photographer wants something, listen to him – he's spent years with people who are uncomfortable in front of a camera, he knows what to do. In this case, the news reporter asked leading questions, which is bad for a politician but good for a writer.

My radio interview was another deal entirely, but also survivable. The main thing you have to remember is that it's live, there's no do over, and if you screw up everyone listening will hear it instantly. So just go out and have fun.

Remember, as a writer, you can't talk. Again, there are exceptions, but most of them are Joss Whedon. Figure out what you may be asked and what you want to say, then write it all down on little index cards.

Your mind *will* go blank.

I thought I was prepared for anything, when I went to the WAWK studio for my interview. I had copies of the book, note cards, I'd used deodorant and brushed my teeth – I was ready. I even showed up half an hour early just in case, so they set me in their conference room, where I passed the time by finding two typos in my brand new book.

Then I started to sniffle.

My throat began to close off. My nose got stuffed up. I began to itch.

Something in the conference room had triggered my allergies. By the time I got into the studio my voice was cracking, I was covered with blotches, and I couldn't breathe. The interviewer started spraying Lysol toward me, so if you hear that noise over the sound my hacking ...

Only you won't, because there wasn't a recording made of the interview. Thank goodness for small favors.

Afterward I stopped at the local pharmacy, as you might imagine, and ran into an old friend. He told me he'd just heard me on the radio, I sounded good (notice he didn't say great), that he was interested in history, and ... here's the important part ... he wanted a copy of the book.

That made the whole thing worthwhile.

THERE'S A STORY AT THE END OF THIS TITLE

There's a burning debate among writers, one that threatens to tear apart our ink-smeared brotherhood:

Chapter titles, or no chapter titles?

Granted, not as exciting as cheese or no cheese if you're *not* a writer, but still. The general consensus in writing for adults is that you don't title your chapters: They should be left with nice, unassuming numbers. This is in case your book is being read by insomniacs, so they can count your chapters and get some sleep.

Much of the modern publishing industry seems to look down at titles, thinking them the mark of amateurish or unserious writing, to which I stick out my tongue and say "nyah!"

I like chapter titles. It's odd, considering how much trouble I have coming up with book titles, but I have a lot of fun titling my chapters. At least I would, if my publisher approved of such a thing.

When I wrote *Smoky Days and Sleepless Nights* I was able to play with the idea, since it's non-fiction. I even went so far as to use subtitles. For instance, Chapter One is:

Life Without a Fire Department

Or,

Who ya' gonna call?

Don't mock me, I was younger then.

I even titled individual passages within chapters. For instance, a section about a fire in an Albion landmark was titled *A Night At The Opera House*, which is hilarious if you've a Marx Brothers fan. If not, it's just ... odd.

Then there was *Fire in Your Drawers,* which was a segment about a fire that broke out in ... well, it seemed funny at the time.

Did any of this affect sales? I dunno. You figure out what affects book sales, and get back to me.

Anyway, when the time came for me to finish *The No-Campfire Girls*, I realize I had a chance to follow my heart and stick in chapter titles. Maybe "follow my heart" is a bit too much. Because part of the proceeds was going to a cause almost as good as my own budget, we decided to self-publish the book, which meant I could do whatever the heck I wanted with it. No publishing gatekeepers! I can put every other paragraph upside down, do the whole book without punctuation, have long blocks of educational description about tree bark, whatever I want! Bwahahaha!

It's lines like that one that tend to lead to horror stories about self-publishing, but never mind that.

Mostly I'm a traditionalist when it comes to written storytelling, so none of that other stuff happened (although I am thinking of an experimental short story in which every other sentence is in parenthesis). However, chapter titles are a lot more accepted in young adult literature. I didn't mean *The No-Campfire Girls* to be young adult, mind you ... but the main character is a fifteen year old girl, most of the other characters are teenagers, and the book is set in a girl's camp, so ... there you go.

I still don't really think of it that way, but if a story told by a teenage girl doesn't sound like a teenage girl's story, something's very wrong.

So, yeah, I put in chapter titles. It was fun, and above all else I wanted the story to be fun. Otherwise, why read it? There's no test. It's not on the required reading list at Harvard. (It isn't, is it?)

So—and you are the first people who haven't read the book to know this, if you haven't read the book—here are the chapter titles to *The No-Campfire Girls:*

> *A Burning Ambition*
> *Dress For Protest Success*
> *Half Cherokee, Half Bull*
> *A Cunning Plan*
> *What Could Possibly Go Wrong?*
> *Welcome to The Jungle*
> *Hawkeye and Green Arrow All Rolled Into One*
> *Family Matters*
> *That Went Well*
> *Rotten Ronnie*
> *Totally Not An Emergency*
> *SyFy Original: Fire Tornado*
> *Helter Shelter (This one is my wife's favorite)*

Weathering The Storm
That Can't Be Good
The Cavalry, Not To The Rescue
The Camp Inipi Hotshots
Ditch Digging
Best Session Ever

No, the titles don't necessarily give away plot details. Remember, as my daughters once complained, I can be ironic, sneaky, and just plain mean. Or did I say that about them?

So what do you think? Chapter titles or no chapter titles? Remember, this won't be my last self-published work, and I'm just itchin' for some word play.

LULLABIES ON MY E-BOOKS

There's a certain sense of deja vu in the ongoing debate about whether e-books will spell the end of the written book. I realize there are some people who don't realize books are still being published at all, but I'm guessing most of them don't read this column, anyway.

My publisher—after three years and three books I still have trouble believing I have a publisher—specializes mostly in e-books. For those of you who assumed a nuclear war would happen in the 80s and are just now emerging from their fallout shelters, e-books are electronic books that you can read on a computer, tablet, or phone. I'll let someone else explain how you can read on a phone (ed: get the Kindle app (free) or purchase the HTML or PDF versions of the book and use your web browser of choice).

In the case of my first publisher, if the author wants his book available in print he/she/it has to make the print run worth the e-book publisher's time by committing to buying fifty copies, thankfully at an author's discount. It's one of those extremely rare cases in which I'm okay with violating the old publishing rule, "money always flows to the author". That's designed to keep desperate writers from falling prey to "vanity" publishers, and I just realized I've been laying way too much uninteresting publishing insider stuff on you people.

I don't have a problem with e-books. I read all the time on my computer, and I've got a Kindle that will fit in my coat pocket, yet still hold hundreds of books. How cool is that? I'm reading a book on my Kindle right now. (Well, not *right* now—right now I'm writing about reading a book on my Kindle right now.)

But as a reader, there's nothing like the heft, feel, even the smell of a printed book. And as a writer, it just doesn't seem real until you see your name right there, on the actual cover of an actually printed actual book.

Also, people like to have books signed by the author. I don't know why, although not knowing why doesn't keep me from owning several autographed books myself. Signing the screen of an e-reader not only doesn't please your reading public, it actually upsets them.

My publisher has set the print price of my newest book at $16.99, which to me seems high for an unknown writer. For people willing to give that much money I'll not only sign it, I'll have my picture taken with it, sing a lullaby to them, and give them a DNA sample.

(Yes, I do think *"The Notorious Ian Grant"* is worth that kind of money. It's a good quality printing and a fun story, and even my speed reading sister takes a whole night to read the book. You'd pay that much at the movies by the time you got past the snack counter, and that's just for a two hour film and forty minutes of trailers. Just the same, I'd have priced it lower—although I am hoping to someday be so successful that my ego becomes a problem.)

I'm sure enough people prefer "real" books that I'll be able to sell my copies. Maybe "sure" isn't the word ... how about "hopeful"? But although I'll make more profit on those than on an e-book sale, as a writer I don't care *how* people read my book ... as long as they do. So to me the whole question of whether an e-book or print book is better is a pointless argument. Go both ways. Duh.

The question that panics people is, will e-books kill print? Okay, that's a bigger question than worrying over my little corner of publishing. However, my answer remains the same: Duh.

Not the most illuminating answer in the world, I know.

Do you remember when the paperback novel killed the hard cover book? No? How about when the internet killed TV? Or when TV killed the movie theater? Or when TV killed radio? Or when radio killed newspapers?

No?

The important thing is to get people reading, and to keep them reading. How doesn't matter. Start them on internet comic strips, trashy romances, cereal boxes, whatever. (Warning: Cereal boxes aren't as fun as they used to be.) Maybe they get excited by the sight of a library, like I do. Or they read on a screen. Or they hear a book on audio. Or they read it on their e-glasses while driving down the highway.

Okay, maybe not that last one.

These days writers can do all sorts of things with an electronic book: add music, photos, even video. Make them interactive. Have them brew your coffee in the morning. Being the more traditional sort, I'm just guessing on the last one. But if it gets your imagination working, gets you into a story, entertains and illuminates, then it's all good.

But just to be clear, I won't really be singing lullabies on my e-books.

IF YOU HAVE FREE TIME, YOU'RE NOT DOING IT RIGHT

Writer/director Joss Whedon (you may have heard of *The Avengers*) once said something that really spoke to me, something that says a lot about my writing career.

He said, "I have a lot of ideas ... it's just a question of free time."

Boy, ain't that the truth. He also said "Be yourself, unless you suck", which also says a lot about my writing career.

The biggest reason I didn't get published twenty years ago is that I just didn't have the free time to plug away at the writing and selling. (*Thirty* years ago it was because I wasn't being myself, and I sucked.) Ideas? Not a problem.

Other writers complain about writer's block, but story ideas swirl around me like mosquitos on a hike. I used to make lists of ideas, dozens of them, in different genres and different lengths. The fact that my first published novel was a romantic comedy was largely a matter of chance. (And the male lead's name is Chance! Coincidence? Well, yes.)

I recently dug up my lists of story ideas. One of the first things I noticed was that I love a good series. I came up with scores of ideas for book series, probably because my first literary love was the Oz books, and there were forty of those.

My first idea for a series was what today we'd call space opera: Science fiction involving space travel along with nice, fun, death and destruction. Sometime in my mid-teens I developed a story universe involving the crew of a space ship, who would travel around the galaxy exploring strange new worlds, seeking out new life forms and new civilizations, boldly going ...

Yeah, it was a *Star Trek* rip-off, although my conscious brain didn't realize that until years later. So I completely overhauled the whole concept, changing the characters and situations around so they were unrecognizable from my originals. My new captain was an older, cerebral type; my first officer was the adventurous lady killer; my ship's doctor was female; and my science officer was still alien, but wanted to experience emotions and understand humanity.

Then *Star Trek: The Next Generation* started airing.

That was one of my first lessons in fiction: Creative minds think alike, so if you just hold onto your ideas, someone else is likely to do them first. Or, Gene Rodenberry broke into my closet late one night.

Meanwhile, I came up with an idea for a series of books set in a fictional city, about brave and daring firefighters who – wait for it – fight fires. While my space opera tales were mostly short stories, I completed rough drafts of a dozen novel length manuscripts about my intrepid, and boring, firefighters.

Yeah, they were boring, especially the main character. He was so sincere and earnest that, once I gained some experience in character creation, I just wanted to slap him. My firefighters had no quirks, no bad habits, and they never, ever failed. Those are the people you want showing up for emergencies in real life, but not in stories. So I overhauled that fictional universe too, and later on started a new story that, if I do say so myself, was not only more interesting but a lot more realistic. Gotta get around to finishing that.

Along the way I came up with an idea for a dystopian type trilogy ... this was back before trilogies became the big buzz word in both novels and movies. It was about a group of intrepid adventurers (I'm detecting a pattern) who set out across a post-apocalyptical world in a kind of super-RV, searching for a refuge from various bad guys. It really wasn't too bad, considering I completed the first one in high school.

Unfortunately, by the time I wrote the second one I'd been heavily influenced by this brand new movie, *Star Wars*, and my sequel stole all the fun stuff like sword fights, sexy princesses, and fighter battles. If I ever get around to writing the third book, I'll have to go back and remove everything that has a John Williams soundtrack.

I was big into science fiction back then, and jotted down ideas, outlines, story openings and scenes for all sorts of outlandish stuff. The two dozen or so short stories I submitted to magazines back then came zooming back to me at warp speed, a good sign that I was putting the cart (or the starship) before the horse (or the warp drive). I finished one rough draft about a group of teenagers lost on a runaway starship, which maybe would go over with the young adult audience today.

Another completed draft was a farce involving a scavenger hunt in a small town, where things go out of control in an 80's comedy kind of way – the kind of thing you'd find former Saturday Night Live cast members doing. I'm kind of proud of that, actually … I should resurrect its profound silliness someday, and see if I can inject an actual plot into it.

Finally came my most recent idea for a series, a comic mystery that evolved into a young adult story without my knowledge, and holds great potential for things to come. I named the story *Red is for "Ick"*, with the theory that each subsequent book could have a color in the title. Hey, it works for other mystery writers … numbers, letters, dress sized, whatever.

After all that, is it any wonder I'm surprised to find my first publication turned out to be a romance? What doesn't surprise me, considering my history, is the demand by those who read it for a sequel … another series, maybe, assuming the sales of the first one and its accompanying short story collection are high enough. (*Mark's note: The sequel,* The Notorious Ian Grant, *came out in 2014.*)

So where do I go next? Science fiction? Action-adventure? Musical comedy?

I've got lots of ideas … it's just a matter of free time. Darn that modern society, and its demand that I actually earn a living until then.

WITH A NICE GARLAND OF GARLAND SAUCE

What the hell is garland, anyway?

Please excuse my language; this is not one of the columns I wrote for the newspaper, and so I can in theory say whatever the heck I want. I can in fact say stuff that would put me on the IRS "most audited list", so I'm not going to go there. You hear that, NSA?

Emily wanted garland. For the Christmas tree, I mean. Not garnish. Garland. I suppose you could garnish a tree with garland. Or, you could make garland out of garlic, thus preventing an attack by vampire termites. Yes, you could garnish with garish gobs of garlic garland.

My wife was not impressed when I told her this, and so I had to admit that I didn't really know what garland was. When I was a kid, we used tinsel on the Christmas tree. As it turns out, some say tinsel is a type of garland, but garland is more like a rope, while tinsel is like a bundle of little strings that you throw over the tree, draping said tree with tiny little metallic icicles. Plastic now, of course.

For some reason, it's hard to find tinsel these days. I'm guessing it has to do with the cleanup involved in gathering all those little pieces together for annual storage, except those that get wound around the vacuum cleaner beater bar and have to be dug out with scissors and cursing. That's worthy of a "hell".

Worst case scenario involves digging it out of your cat. That's worthy of way more than a "hell".

I pointed out to my wife that we already had a little Garland figurine on the bookcase, and she pointed back that she was talking about the decoration, not the Wizard Of Oz.

But I knew what she was really talking about. While Christmas garland is only one type of garland, when you ask for it after Thanksgiving everyone pretty much knows what you're talking about. Not so with garnish, by the way. And it turns out I was also familiar with garland, because when I was a kid we actually did make it out of strings and popcorn. If my parents had added butter and salt, I'd have been in big trouble.

These days the typical Christmas garland is made out of—wait for it—plastic. Just like tinsel, which is garland. But we got some anyway, and it looks pretty good.

Doesn't smell good, though. I can't decide whether to add garlic or salt and butter.

This is not garland. This is a mustache.

PART FIVE:

how do you spell miscellaneous?

The great thing about being a humor columnist is that you don't have to concentrate on one specific subject. If you can make fun of it, it's open season. Even if you can't make fun of it, you can make fun of it. Nothing's sacred, unless you write a newspaper column, which I did.

(Mark's note: After I wrote this opening, terrorists attacked a satirical newspaper in France and proved something I've always suspected: People who can't take a joke are both crazy and dangerous.)

So, what did I not write about? Well ... sex, for one thing, and even then I'd occasionally slip it in. Otherwise, I touched on pretty much everything, including stuff that made me and probably my readers uncomfortable. Politics, religion, death ... and some stuff that couldn't really be categorized. If it couldn't be categorized it probably wasn't timely, which meant it hid in my extra file until ... now.

NOTHING CAN SINK THIS - NEVER MIND

Would you book passage on the *Titanic II*?

Yeah, me neither. And yet an Australian rich guy still plans to rebuild an exact replica of the ill-fated liner, hopefully not including sappy love stories or gaping holes in the hull.

The original *Titanic* was the most luxurious ride around, if you were rich, up to and including first seat on the lifeboats. If you weren't rich it was similar to that first apartment you had after school—the one where the dining room was one corner of the kitchen, you could reach out and touch both bathroom walls, and the sound on your black and white TV would only work if you perched heavy weights on one end.

Wait ... that was *my* first apartment. At least my walls didn't leak.

The thing is, Clive Palmer isn't planning a ship that just looks like the one that went to the bottom a century ago: He wants an exact duplication, right down to the really, really lousy steerage class. The cabins really were the size of my first apartment, which is not a compliment. Bathrooms were shared by your closest two dozen neighbors, meals consisted of the not-very-best boiled potatoes, and if you wanted ice in your drink ... well, you'd better hope for no ice.

I assume they'll make a few safety related changes. Then again, if human race is capable of anything, it's repeating the mistakes of the past.

If they charge the same as the original *Titanic*, adjusted for inflation, you could cross the Atlantic in steerage for only a thousand dollars or so. Isn't that great for traveling below sea level in a space the size of Scooby-Doo's van? On the other hand, some Americans have already offered a million bucks to be on the maiden voyage, giving foreigners yet another good reason to make fun of Americans.

Palmer said the experience would be so realistic that travelers will get 1920's period costumes, which is only funny when you realize the original *Titanic* had been on the bottom of the Atlantic for years before the 20's hit. Also, they might get hosed down with confetti as a way of demonstrating the de-lousing process because, after all, there were no lice in America. Oh, come on ... I thought you said this would be realistic? Next you'll be telling us they'll have enough lifeboats.

The good news: Star-crossed, movie style doomed romances will not be allowed.

You may think this is distasteful. Nope – we need to raise the bar on distaste, because, also scheduled to open in 2016, is a theme park in Central China. This theme park will be anchored by a *Titanic* museum and ...

Shipwreck simulator.

This is at a theme park 930 miles from the nearest ocean, by the way, which may give visitors a false sense of security. The boss of the investment group building the park said, according to Yahoo! News:

"We think it's worth spreading the spirit of the *Titanic*."

The spirit of the Titanic? You mean the spirit of poor planning leading to multiple deaths? I can get you that spirit all over the world.

"The universal love and sense of responsibility shown during the Titanic shipwreck represented the spiritual richness of human civilization."

Clearly this guy didn't see the same movie I did. He also said Asia needs its own Titanic museum, which I found odd. I'm not seeing the direct connection, here. It would be like Kansas building a Mount Vesuvius Museum.

Several hundred people at a time will board the simulation, and sink.

Well, not literally, I assume. They're using sound and lighting effects, and apparently a really big ice sculpture. People will walk away from it thinking, "So that's what it's like being on a big ship stranded on land when an earthquake hits. Pass the ice, my drink is getting warm."

I suppose you think this is the most ridiculous *Titanic* related thing you've ever heard of.

Oh, no. That's just the tip of the iceberg. (Yeah, I said it.)

In 2010 a movie came out: *Titanic II*. Yep. Beating Palmer to the tacky punch, *Titanic II* told the story of a new luxury liner, called the—well, you know—which is hit by an iceberg.

But this is Hollywood. Let's punch it up a bit, shall we? Let's have it start sinking after a *tsunami* hurls the iceberg into our intrepid new ship!

I'll admit I haven't watched it. But as disaster movies go, that one would have to be a disaster.

THEY'RE DYING TO GET IN

Where do you expect to go when you die?

Well, I hope to go into a box at Rose Hill Cemetery, just across town. This would be preferable to, say, having your preserved body being put on display as a war criminal, getting buried in a serial killer's basement, or being eaten by dingoes.

But what happens to your body isn't important compared to what happens to your soul. Heaven? Hell? The same place as all those missing socks? Despite all the worries of life, afterlife remains an area of concern. In fact, a Harris Poll called America "a nation of believers". Can you believe that?

I found the results surprising, starting with the opening statement that "most Christians, not surprisingly, believe in God."

What? Huh? Hold up the ark there, fella. *Most* Christians believe in God? How the heck can you be a Christian and not believe in God? Isn't that the point?

"Oh, I don't really believe, but I like the songs and those tasty wafers."

As if that wasn't enough, more than a quarter of those who say they're *not* Christians believe in the Virgin birth and the resurrection of Jesus. Maybe they just don't want to follow some of that other stuff in the Bible, like being a decent person and not cheating on your taxes. (Someone will point out, correctly, that there's stuff in the Bible that most modern Christians don't buy, but I'm not here to start any scholarly arguments.)

That's the problem with polls: People who answer them always hedge their bets. For instance, 90% of the people believe in God, while 89% believe in miracles. Does 1% of the population believe there's a God who can't work miracles? That's like believing there's a Chef Gordon Ramsay who can't curse.

How, then, do you explain rainbows? Hummingbirds? The fact that ice floats? Seriously – other liquids sink when they turn to solid, which would give ice skating a way higher degree of difficulty.

84% of people believe the soul survives after death, which mean 16% think when it's over, it's over. Then what's your reward for being good, or your punishment for being bad? Are we to understand that Mother Teresa got no frequent giver miles? For that matter, why have I been holding doors open for people all those years?

69% believe in hell, but 68% believe in the devil. That means 1% of people think there's a hell, but no one's in charge. Eternal torture without organization, like Black Friday at Wal-Mart.

51% believe in ghosts. I consider myself open minded, but what are the rules? If everyone becomes a ghost, why aren't they overwhelming the world? Can you imagine what a city as old as London would look like? If not everyone becomes a ghost, how is the choice made? Dice? Raffle? Psychiatric evaluation?

And is it a punishment, or a reward? After all, wouldn't it be kind of fun to mess with the living?

Too many questions, which may explain why 31% believe in astrology. Being a fan of astronomy, I know that the planets and stars hold their courses and don't physically affect Earth much ... but then, I would think that way, being a Cancer.

27% believe in reincarnation, but that number is driven up by their past selves. Oddly, they all claim to be someone famous. They were Caesar, Jefferson, William the Conqueror – you can't *all* have been Joan of Ark. Somebody – in fact, most people – had to be the lowly and unknown soldiers who followed her.

So I don't buy it. When hypnotists start doing regressions to past lives and hear, "Wait, I'm just an unknown teenage British sailor! And I'm dying of typhoid!", then I'll rethink my stance.

When those polled are asked where they expect to go when they die, the answers are pretty much as expected. 63% assume they'll go to Heaven, which is quite an assumption. These are people with high degrees of self-confidence, and I can't help thinking some are in for an unpleasant surprise. In fact, I suspect those who think they don't deserve to go to Heaven may be the ones most likely to make it.

1% expect to go to Hell. Now, if those people are so convinced, shouldn't they be the first ones to make some lifestyle changes? If you're absolutely positive you're going to be standing in a lake of fiery brimstone, poked by demons with pitchforks, and forced to listen to rap-polka-elevator music for eternity, wouldn't you try to avoid it?

6% think they'll go to purgatory, which is much like the Newark Airport.

11% expect to go someplace else. Where? We've been through all the normal choices. The rings of Saturn? A Justin Beiber concert? Or would that take us back to purgatory?

Here's the honest answer: You can't know where you're going, not for sure. You can only have faith and hope. No matter how good you are, you can't get to Heaven through words or deeds, but through acceptance that the choice belongs to someone else – and that's an idea that scares a lot of people to d – um, scares a lot of people.

So the truth is really with that 18% of people who admitted that they didn't have a clue. Personally, I think that percentage must be much higher.

I'm totally going to change my name before I die.

A MAIL NAMED SUE

Q: What do you call a hundred lawyers on a one-way trip to the Moon?

A: A good start.

The legal profession is one of those few groups that, as a whole, it's still okay for everyone to hate and put down. PC be damned (excuse me, darned), they join one of those rare groups that everyone can swear at and make fun of without raising an eyebrow, right alongside Congressmen, Christians, and mimes.

Don't get me *started* on mimes.

I have a reputation for hating lawyers. As a group it isn't true – one of the most decent human beings I ever met in my life was a lawyer who became a judge – but I write 52 columns a year: I have to make fun of *somebody*.

The truth is that attorneys, like Christians, are as a group decent, hardworking people who contribute to society and care about what they're doing. (Notice I didn't mention Congressmen.) Mimes ... well, they're just evil, like tarantulas and fried liver.

But lawyers, like Christians and even mimes, can be made to look bad by the actions of a few of their members. Or, in the case of Congressmen, a lot of their members.

There are two groups who make lawyers look particularly bad: Ambulance chasers and, of course, Congressmen.

I now have some personal experience with ambulance chasers.

Back in October, while I drove through a parking garage in Fort Wayne, a young man backed out of his spot and into my car. It caused about $1,500 damage to my car and left Emily and me with very slight injuries, which we didn't mention to the kid who hit us because he was upset enough as it was.

He apologized, admitted his fault, called his parents, stayed until the police arrived – all those things you're supposed to do. We turned it over to his insurance, they made some inquiries, and eventually they cut us a check for the repairs. That's it. It was a fender bender, these things happen.

Within days of the accident, I started getting letters. Letters from lawyers.

It turns out "We're here to work for *you*" actually means "We're here to *sue* for you, and our percentage."

One of them sent me an entire freaking packet in a manila envelope, complete with a 25 page, full color brochure. Now, keep in mind the accident happened in Fort Wayne: this law firm works out of Indianapolis.

"According to police reports we have examined, you were involved in an accident on October 21st, at which time you may have suffered an injury that warrants the assistance and representative of a qualified lawyer."

There are law firms all across the state that employ people to go around looking at crash reports, in the hopes of suing some poor college kid who just had his first accident.

The letter went on for two entire pages, single spaced, in addition to the pamphlet. *Seventeen* attorneys were listed as members of this law firm, ready to come to my home and initiate their own investigation in which I won't be charged unless they get a recovery. Oh, how nice. No risk to me.

But it was his fault, you say. Yes, it was. He had an insurance company, as required by law, and they made it right to the extent of getting us a rental car while mine was being fixed. No lawyers necessary. If the lawyers had come in, well – it's just an insurance company that gets hit, right? Just the giant, evil Big Insurance that will suck up the costs, and certainly they wouldn't raise rates to cover their costs.

People, *that* is why our insurance rates are so high. Ambulance chasers, frivolous lawsuits, greed, and a Congress that passed a Godzilla of a healthcare law that stomps around the countryside, at no point actually addressed the question of tort reform.

Had to get a dig in at Congress, there; it's been nine paragraphs.

I'm not saying attorneys aren't necessary for going after the truly evil out there, the grossly negligent, the criminal, or the mimes. I'm just saying maybe the insurance industry isn't the only group that's making the cost of health care go up. Maybe it's time to take a long, hard look at the actions of those lawyers who let greed be their guide, with the result that the people of America have become both poorer and more paranoid of doing right, for fear of being found wrong.

Also, Congress stinks, and maybe we should replace the lawyers in that institution with mimes. At the very least, there'd be a lot fewer dumb things being said.

BECAUSE "MIMEME" IS LONG, AND SO IS MY UNDERWEAR

Do you know what "meme" is?

Me neither, so I looked it up on that paragon of accuracy, Wikipedia. Turns out it's a shortened version of "mimeme", an ancient Greek word meaning something imitated, or to imitate, or in this case maybe to irritate. Is that cool, or what?

From an internet standpoint, it originally meant an idea that propagated through the web, often in the form of a question and answer quiz that you're supposed to fill out, then pass along to all your friends. These days it's also an image, video, picture, hashtag—don't get me started on hashtags—that gets so popular it temporarily overshadows the latest Hollywood scandal. You know, the one about the celebrity and drugs, or sex, or an auto accident while having sex on drugs.

I was sent an underwear meme.

Seems a bit personal? Well, that's the nature of memes. Many of them are designed so that people who become friends on the internet get to know more personal details about each other, just as they would if they became friends in real life and, say, sat around talking about their underwear. 'Cause that's what me and my friends always sat around doing.

"Say, you try them new Fruit of the Looms?"

"Yep, they seemed a bit binding."

No, I never took it easy around the poker table, drinking a beer and discussing my underwear. Not only did I have no desire to, but frankly it didn't seem like the kind of thing my friends would like to hear. In fact, I was going to fill the meme out as if written by one of my book characters. I thought that would be more interesting and less embarrassing, not to mention the idea that the more a writer knows about their characters, the better he can write them in a story.

I'm not sure I buy that on an underwear basis, but we'll see.

Still, it only seems fair: Others of my friends were being up front about underneath, so shouldn't I be? So here, for the first time: All about my underwear. Make the kids turn away.

What do you call your underwear/undergarments? Do you have any commonly used nicknames for them?

In a word, no. What, people nickname their *underwear*?

"Yeah, let me put on Slim Jim and I'll be right there."

"Honey, have you seen Eddie Elastic?"

I don't think so. I call my underwear ... well ... underwear.

Have you ever had that supposedly common dream of being in a crowded place in only your underwear?

113

Sadly, yes. Speaking as a person who rarely wears shorts and has been made fun of for not taking off my shoes in my own home, I can tell you I wouldn't be thrilled to be running around publicly in my tighty whities, or even my Pink Power Ranger pajamas. (What? She was my favorite.)

My dream usually involves not only being in my underwear, but walking around the school in my underwear, unable to find my classroom or books, and realizing I'm late for a class I didn't prepare for. There's usually some falling involved, too.

In other words, my dreams aren't all that much fun.

What is the worst thing you can think of to make underwear out of?

Poison ivy-laced steel wool. I find the fact that I can imagine that to be extremely disturbing.

If you were a pair of panties, what color would you be?

Um ... red from embarrassment? Or pink, I guess, since that's my general skin color. Guess what – these questions get stranger, as tends to happen with memes.

Hm ... why do they call panties a "pair", but bras singular?

Have you ever thrown your underwear at a rock star or other celebrity? If so, which one(s)? If not, which one(s) would you throw your underwear at, given the opportunity?

Former Secretary of State Madeleine Albright. Have you seen her? I'd be very surprised if Bill Clinton never hit on that.

Yeah ... no. I've never understood the point of celebrity crushes to begin with, although I do admit to having something of a man crush on talk show host Craig Ferguson, and his stirring Scottish brogue. (And Sean Connery, come to think of it ... maybe it's the accent.)

I guess I can understand the possibility that some male celebrities may appreciate the underwear toss, assuming they don't get knocked over by a girdle or a pair of granny panties. However, I can't imagine any female celebrity being impressed by some guy hurtling his boxers onto a stage, which would most likely cause *her* to hurl. And not her underwear.

You're out of clean underwear. What do you do?

I always keep an emergency stash of older underwear in the back of the drawer, just in case. No, I do *not* go commando. I only saw the movie *There's Something About Mary* once, but it left an indelible impression on me, so I always keep a layer of cloth between any zipper and my ... self. If you haven't seen the movie, you can probably guess by context what I'm talking about.

Are you old enough to remember Underroos? If so, did you have any?

Underroos, for the uninitiated, were underwear that had the pattern of a superhero costume on them. You could be Batman, Superman,

115

or if you were a girl, Wonder Woman. Or if you were a boy too, I guess, but then you'd face the possibility of your parents sending you into therapy. I never had them, but I now own a fetching Batman ... never mind.

I just Googled "Underoos". Note to self: Tighten up that adult filter setting.

If you could have any message printed on your underwear, what would it be?

"Have you seen my classroom? Can I borrow your notes?"

How many bloggers does it take to put panties on a goat?

Um ... huh?

There's always one last weird, unrelated question tacked onto these memes, just to make people do a double take. I'm not sure how PETA feels about forcing animals into human underwear, but the goat's bound to be displeased.

By the way, the actual number of bloggers it takes is 42. It may seem like a lot, but bloggers are generally an out of shape bunch, and the goats can get *very* displeased.

IT'S GOT DOS!

It's a word processor and printer in one machine—and it's got DOS!

Ah, the good old days.

Every ten years or so, I clean out my basement. Sometimes that turns up interesting things, alive and dead. This time I found the box my very first portable word processor came in.

No, not computer—word processor.

My Canon Star Writer 300 went to that Great Electronic Junk Pile in the Sky years ago, after its built-in printer and amazing floppy disk system gave up the ghost in the machine. But looking at the box made me realize just how much technology really improved over the years.

In middle school, I wrote (not very good) stories of action/adventure and science fiction daring with ... a pencil. And paper, of course. In high school I graduated to a pen, my first upgrade. Then, I took the second most important class of high school:

Typing.

Surely there must have been a more important class, but that's the one that had the biggest impact on my life.

Not keyboarding, mind you—I'm talking big electric typewriters. I learned QWERTY, touch typing, and of course how to use carbon paper so I'd always have a backup copy.

When I graduated, my mother gave me her old manual typewriter. A step backward, but power outages were no problem. I wore out three manuals while writing (bad) short stories, novel rough drafts, and my early columns.

You might need to ask your grandmother what a manual typewriter is. Go ahead, I'll wait.

I know, amazing that there's no power cord, huh? Well, I brought myself into the 20th Century around 1990, with a desktop word processor.

No, not computer.

But why did I need a computer? I was a writer. Writers don't need computers! I had a bookshelf full of dictionaries, thesauruses (is that how you spell that?) and encyclopedias. Still, it sure was nice to be able to edit on that word processor screen.

Anyone my age or younger can guess how quickly I became addicted to that word processor. I could *edit on the screen*. Then I could push a button and print it out. Naturally I didn't just save my work on one of those newfangled, untrustworthy floppy disks.

The only problem was, I couldn't carry it around and write anywhere, the way I could with a pen and notebook. So in the mid-90's I found an alternative: a *portable* word processor. I had two choices: One had a battery but had to be connected to a remote printer, and the other had to be plugged in, but had an onboard printer.

Why in the world would anyone need a battery?

I loved my Star Writer 300 (which I assume isn't for sale anymore, so I can say the name). I wrote hundreds of articles, dozens of columns, and several novels on it. When I hit the print button, they were ready: No marking them up with red ink, no proofreader's marks, no correction fluid or erasing pencil. It was a freaking miracle of modern technology.

That was only two dozen years ago.

Those of you even less tech-savvy than me, try to follow along. Those of you who know your computerized stuff may start uncontrollably giggling. Because, although my Star Writer 300 didn't have a battery, here's some of the stuff it did have:

Over 75 clip art images!

Five fonts. *Five!* Who would ever need more than five? Also five type sizes, and five shading patterns – when you put all that together with normal, bold, underline, italic, and outline styles, you had over 700 print variations. The mind boggles.

A spell checker corrector built-in. Did you *hear* that? It checks the spelling *itself*! (However, spell checking a novel took forever.)

And it takes 3.5 inch floppy disks! And has a DOS screen! And you can fit *thirty sheets* of paper at a time into that printer! It truly was, as advertised, a "personal publishing system".

There were other neat little items, such as multilingual capabilities, search and replace, and word count—I actually had a pre-computer letter to the editor published in Writer's Digest Magazine about how to calculate word counts in a manuscript. That's how complicated it could get, back then.

All this in a compact, 7.4 pound package. The cost: $249.00.

I'm not making fun of it. On the contrary, it was a wonderful machine, just as the Model T was, and the rotary phone. It's just amazing that two decades later there's a thousand times more computer power in my phone than there was in that device.

Things change. Things change so much, that the Star Writer 300 has been repurposed. In researching this column, I discovered a model exactly like mine for sale on eBay, with this attractive selling point:

"This WP would help prepare and store documents under absolute privacy without fears of being under any surveillance."

In other words, since it's incapable of going online or communicating with modern technology, it's free of everything from malware to NSA bugs. Well, that's just brilliant. Call it nostalgic paranoia.

WITH TWO YOU GET DINOSAUR EGG ROLL

My wife is very clear in her conviction that she is never, *never*, going to have kids. I'm cool with this. I had two kids with my first wife, and spent the next quarter of a century exhausted. Now I have two grandkids, which tells me I'm going to spend another quarter of a century exhausted.

My grandkids are twins. Double the exhaustion, double the cost. The good news is they aren't identical, so I don't have to make excuses for why I can't tell them apart.

Now, being a person who never, *never* wants to have kids, you'd think Emily wouldn't want to spend any time around kids. This may someday be a deciding factor between my dueling desires to be near my family, yet move to someplace where snow is a vague, uncertain concept. She wants to live in south Florida? Oh, well … guess I'll wind Christmas lights around our orange trees and text a photo to the freezing relatives.

Being that we're both winter haters, I was hardly surprised the other day to see her perusing for-sale home listings. Where, I wondered? Arizona? Hawaii? Downtown Hades?

"Look at this house!" she said. "It has two bathrooms—not half of one like our house—and a fenced in back yard for the kids and dog."

Wait, kids?

So I looked at the listing. Instead of a thousand miles away near the Gulf Stream, it was in Kendallville, twelve miles from our Albion home. Believe me, twelve miles doesn't make one bit of weather distance in Northern Indiana. At least, not once you're out of the lake effect snow band.

"But ... why would you want to move to Kendallville?" I asked her.

"Well, we could be closer to the twins."

This from the woman who hit me whenever I called her "grandma".

I never really considered that Emily would worry about my offspring and off-offspring as much as I do. But then, I also never considered that after my kids moved out on their own I'd continue worrying about them just as much as when they were kids. I never considered a lot of things, considering I also once swore I'd never have kids, and the only thing I can tell you is that in the end, it's totally worth it.

Anyway, I should have seen it coming. Emily was a counselor in training, and then a counselor, at a Girl Scout camp. You don't do a job like that for more than one summer if you don't like being around kids. So it wasn't really a shock the first time she got that sad-eyed face and said, "I miss the twins."

"Well, I do too, but there's a snow plow stuck in a drift outside."

Next thing I knew, my wife was baking toy dinosaurs into a pan of wet soil, so the three of them could practice archeology. She used to make me brownies in those pans. My palate is confused, but let's face it—they're loveable as all get-out. (The twins, not the dinosaur brownies.)

Next thing I know my wife, who has long talked of owning a place in the country where she can have horses, is discussing the advantages of buying a house in the middle of a city of 10,000, so the twins can walk from their house to our house. Or at least something only a few miles away, so they could come over to ride horses.

Maybe we'll just have a winter home in Florida.

Dude, how can you not remember me? We were womb mates!

PART SIX:

part two of the writer's life
or:
six into two makes... something

Sometimes people ask me what the most surprising part of being a published novelist is. That's easy: The surprising part is that very little has actually changed for me. Same job, same house, same car, and the same income, which is less than if my job consisted of the words "Welcome to Wal-Mart".

That's after five books, unless you include the anthologies I took part in—then it's seven. If you're holding this in your hand, it's eight. Do I get recognized on the street? Occasionally, but not because of my fancy new sports car.

(Say ... am I old enough now to buy a sports car and blame it on a midlife crisis? I'm thinking red Mustang convertible.)

I can only remember one time when a stranger recognized my name as a novelist, and believe me: Once I got out of earshot, I squealed way more than she did.

THE LONG AND THE SHORT OF IT

Although coming up with 52 ideas a year can be a chore – especially come winter, when laughing hysterically can turn into hysterical laughter – this column is the most enjoyable paying job I've ever had. (I never got any paying customers for my walk-through supermodel body wash idea. I mean, walking is what they do, right?)

Or it *was* my favorite job, until the first time somebody handed over cash for a copy of my first novel. At that point fiction writing became my favorite paying job, where before it had been my favorite hobby time-suck. Sure, I haven't made enough to pay back the cost of my first word processor, but I'm a by-gosh *author*.

The *worst* writing job is a miserable chore for a novelist: the synopsis.

A synopsis is a short description of your work, kind of like the back cover blurb. Depending on what the editor wants, some run ten pages or more, but one or two pages is more common. In one page, you have to boil down your epic 300,000 word other-world fantasy, putting in plot, setting, major characters and events, and the ending, while also demonstrating your amazing writing ability.

Recently I was in a writing contest that required me to boil my novel down to one hundred words.

One. Hundred. Words. The novel is 60,000 words long.

I did it because, hey – I wanted to enter. (No, I didn't win.) Just about every fiction author has to do some version of this: Even self-published authors usually have to write blurbs and advertisements. But frankly, the thought of boiling *Gone With the Wind* down to a hundred words would have sent Margaret Mitchell into a sobbing fetal position on the veranda. *War and Peace?* You lost three percent of your space just writing down the title, bub.

But that's part of the job. I've had hundreds of novel ideas over the years, in a half dozen different genres. Could I get each novel idea out in just a hundred words? Pitching a story to editors and agents has become increasingly popular, and who knows who I'll meet in an elevator? Or stand next to in the men's room? (At which point they probably would rather I not talk, but still.)

You have to be careful how you write it, though. If you're not, your synopsis can come out sounding like a completely different story. For instance, here's a famous blurb Rick Polito wrote in 1998:

"Transported to a surreal landscape, a young girl kills the first person she meets and then teams up with three strangers to kill again."

That is, of course, *The Wizard of Oz*.

So here's a blurb I wrote for my novel *The Notorious Ian Grant*:

When infamous party boy and b-list celebrity Ian Grant learns his sister is marrying a cop, he drives straight to Indiana. His plan: to make up for all those times he embarrassed his family by taking charge of the wedding planning. So, Ian's never planned a wedding ... how hard could it be?

Hurricane, Indiana, is a world Ian wouldn't mind being part of, if only people would stop judging him by his previous antics. He might even have a shot at romance with his future brother-in-law's coworker, detective Fran Vargas. But for Fran everything's gone wrong since the moment Ian arrived, including their confrontation with a bullying politician, and an influx of nosy reporters and angry ex-girlfriends. Plus, Ian's wedding planning keeps getting interrupted by someone trying to kill him.

No one ever said redemption is easy.

Not that bad, and accurate—but 38 words over the limit. Now, I could have written it like this:

The beleaguered town of Hurricane, Indiana, already struggling to recover from a natural disaster, is invaded by a mysterious stranger who brings destruction wherever he goes. Police detective Fran Vargas fights politics and red tape as she investigates Ian Grant, who claims to be there to help. But someone has followed him, and as Fran tries to uncover which side Ian is on, she soon finds herself and her friends in harm's way.

Exact same story. Completely different feel. It's like the way you can edit a trailer for the same movie to make it look like a light comedy, or a horror film.

That's the way it is in the writing biz. If I want to sell my story, I have to keep the feel of what I wrote, and still be accurate ... all in a hundred words. It's probably less stressful than being a brain surgeon, but also pays a lot less.

SO, YOU WANT TO BE A NOVELIST

I first wrote this article for a writing blog, but I thought I'd throw it in for those of you who might be would-be writers. By the way, don't be would-be writers. Be writers, or do something more fun and less stressful.

Okay, so you're ready to start your novel ...

Aren't you?

I started mine on January 2nd, with the goal of writing around 5,000 words a week and having the first draft finished by spring. But I planned that start for weeks. Let's take a look at what might – or might not – work for you.

Which comes first, character or the plot? Well, you can't go far without figuring that out, but the answer is a matter of opinion. I start with a plot idea:

"What would happen if a photographer from California arrived in rural Indiana predicting an oncoming storm, only to lock horns with a cop who hates photographers – and Californians?"

That one sentence began a yearlong project that eventually turned into my first published novel, *Storm Chaser*. For the sequel, I started out with another basic question:

"What if the photographer's infamous ne'er-do-well brother heard about his sister's new relationship, and determined to be her wedding planner as a way of making up with her—despite having absolutely no experience in wedding planning?"

"And what then?" (Oh, come on – *Storm Chaser* is a romantic comedy: Surely it's not a spoiler to say the story ended with a new relationship? It's all about how they got there.)

In the end, plot based stories often begin with "What if?" followed by "What then?"

Character based stories, on the other hand, often begin with—wait for it—a strong character:

"Fran Vargas-Mendoza is a no-nonsense cop who worked her way past sexism and racism to become a young Indiana State Police detective. A third generation Mexican-American, she's become popular around town for her cheeriness and optimism, but has sacrificed her personal life in favor of her job."

Okay, we have the basics of our character. Now what? Maybe the next step will be to ask, "What would happen if the straitlaced Fran encountered legendary bad boy Ian Grant, who seems determined to screw up the life of her new friend, the photographer?"

There, in two sentences, you have the base of my entire *Storm Chaser* sequel, *The Notorious Ian Grant,* despite the fact that I then fill it out with a two page long (single spaced) outline.

Oh, yeah … the outline.

To outline or not to outline? There's a question that could cause fist fights at writer's conferences. "Pantsers" are loud and clear: Outlines constrict them. These people simple start out, and see where the path leads them.

I tried that approach. If you want proof, I give you an entire box full of half-completed manuscripts.

However, for some people it does work, and more power to them. If you decide to outline, how should you do it?

Any way you want. I don't have roman numerals, capital letters, and so on. I just jot down the events of the story in order, sometimes throwing in specific scenes and even quotes, sometimes leaving it very spare and basic. You don't have to use some specific format, this isn't going to be turned in to your English teacher – it's just for you. If a page of scribbling works, fine. If you like a detailed, numbered, scene by scene breakdown, that's fine too.

It's just a guideline, and my stories frequently stray from it as the characters come alive and new ideas pop up. But even if I decide to choose an entirely different path, the finish line is there to guide me on my way.

Speaking of characters coming alive, I like to fully create my characters before I start on the outline, in case they grab me by the short hairs and tell me they're not going the direction I want. Some writers say they have complete control over their characters at all time; but if I do my job right they come alive for me, and sometimes they'll tell me they just wouldn't do what was in my original plan. So, in that way characters trump outline.

What do I know about my characters before I start? Their looks, all their family and friend relationships, their job, past jobs, past loves, pets, desires, dreams, fears, favorite and least favorite seasons, foods, cars, books, TV shows, movies, hobbies, what's in their underwear drawers ...

Well, the list goes on and on. Do a search for "creating characters", or get a book on characterization, and you'll find all sorts of good lists. By the time you're done, you should know not only what they look like and how they'd react in any situation, but every little thing about them, no matter how seemingly insignificant.

Most of this your reader will never learn about. Research should be like an iceberg, with most of it never seen – just the same, research the heck out of each and every person in your story, unless they're a minor character, and sometimes even then.

So, you've got your plot idea, your characters, and your outline. What else? That's the big stuff, other than stocking up on the caffeinated drink of your choice. For *Storm Damage* (*Mark's note: That's the one published as* The Notorious Ian Grant) most of my characters were already created, but I went back and looked through their files. I also had to keep a timeline and a separate page of clues, because there's a bit of a comic mystery involved in this one.

Since it's set in my home area I don't have to do a lot of location research, but be prepared to have a file (computer, print, or both) to hold any information you need to have on hand. When I set my novel *Radio Red* in northern lower Michigan – a six hour drive away – I collected all the information I could on the area, up to and including maps, tourist flyers, photos, and even video, as well as making several trips up there.

(Northern lower Michigan—that would be as opposed to southern upper Michigan, which would be out of the mitten and into, I suppose, the icicle on the other side of Lake Superior. The map of Michigan can get complicated.)

Research has to include your characters' jobs too, of course. I immersed myself in studying weather for *Storm Chaser*, and used my experience as a part time radio personality to create a main character in *Radio Red*.

This is far from a complete list. There are issues of naming your characters, for instance – that could make for a whole piece by itself. But planning ahead a little, even if you don't want a complete outline, can make the writing itself go a lot faster.

Remember, though: Your rough draft is allowed to stink. If you miss something along the way, or decide you're writing in the wrong tense, or the story goes off the rails, just take a step back (or go for a long walk, or scream into a pillow), then come back and fix things. That's what rough drafts are for.

THE MARK R. HUNTER DRINKING GAME

I got an idea after one of my readers complained that my column was all about me.

My first thought was, "Well, yeah—it's a humor column, and most humor columns are largely about the columnist, if they're not about politics". But it's possible they didn't catch that it's a *humor* column.

It's happened before.

Still, it gave me a great new idea for a game. I call it:

The Mark R. Hunter drinking game.

The first time I heard of the concept was way back with the Sailor Moon drinking game. Sailor Moon is a Japanese anime, the short explanation being it's an animated TV show that was mangled by translators who dumbed it down for American kids. The show's about a group of teenage girls who magically change into outfits featuring extremely short skirts, then use superpowers to beat up on anyone who looks at their legs.

They beat up people a lot.

So the drinking game would involve taking a drink if, for instance, one of the characters changes into their costume onscreen (in a magic, totally not nude—exactly—kind of a way). You'd take a drink if the main character whines. Believe me, she whines a lot. You'd take a drink if the two lesbian characters, who have been turned into "cousins" for American consumption, give each other loving, totally not cousin-like, looks.

You get the idea. Well, you probably don't—it's something you have to experience. The show inexplicably became popular among drinking-age Americans, for reasons that probably have to do with the short skirts, thus the drinking game.

So I thought, okay: If my column is all about me, let's turn *it* into a drinking game. This is, unfortunately, a game I'm bound to lose, as I rarely drink. Also, I'm not sure how you determine the winner. The person who loses consciousness first, or last? Just the same, I've developed my own drinking game to show how often I repeat myself, and whether I can be called egocentric … or possibly just neurotic, like most humorists.

Here's what to watch for in my column, and what to drink if you see it:

If I mention spiders and fear thereof, have a Jell-O shot.

(See how it works?)

If I use parenthesis, have a JagerBomb. (I don't actually know what a JagerBomb is, but I'm sure you'll love it.)

If I mention a mishap during vacation, have Sex On the Beach. It's a drink—get your minds out of the gutter.

If I use a play on words for misdirection, such as the above, that's a shot of whiskey.

If I pun, find something that's good for what *ales* you.

If I mention any book I've written, have a Martini. If I mention it while slyly working in information on how you can buy it, instruct the bartender to give it to you shaken, not stirred, in your best Sean Connery voice. (For instance, if I mention you can find links to my books at **markrhunter.com**.)

If there's any mention at all of a lawn mower exploding or otherwise not working right, it's Margarita time. But remember to hydrate with water before failing to mow.

If I "paraphrase" anything a family member said, have a Brave Bull. This is a drink made from tequila and coffee liqueur, and I use it because I couldn't find a drink with the words "exaggerating what they really said" in the title.

Here's an example of paraphrasing: Suppose my wife comes in and finds some home repair job I was attempting went horribly wrong. In my column, I might paraphrase her as saying, "What have I told you about mixing you and power tools?"

However, in reality she might have said, for example: "Oh, the blood! The blood!" Which wouldn't be as funny. At least, it didn't seem as funny at the time.

If I say something that's not politically correct, have a Dead Nazi. This is a real drink that consists, perhaps not surprisingly, of Jägermeister and Peppermint Schnapps. On a related note, I learned quite a bit about mixed drinks while writing this column.

If I give too much information about my health, you'll find a hard apple cider a day will keep the doctor columns away.

If I make fun of politics, sip a wine cooler. If I zero in on Joe Biden, look for a drink called Nuts and Berries.

If I mention any of our pets, combine coconut rum, melon liqueur, and pineapple juice into a drink called a Scooby Snack.

If I mention, which is to say complain, about the weather, have a Long Island Iced Tea. Have it on a beach in Florida.

If the column is about something going horribly wrong while doing home maintenance, have a Shirley Temple.

Yes, I'm aware that drink is non-alcoholic. Look, I won't be responsible for your blood alcohol level if you slam a shot every time I get scraped, bruised, or shocked. Although it might send *me* to the whiskey.

If I say at any point "what could go wrong?" look up a drink called Sex With an Alligator.

Do you get the feeling they're running out of names for drinks?

And finally, if my column discusses the results of an internet poll or top ten list ... just have a beer.

Why?

Because they're both fillers.

GUESS THE WRITER

This was also not originally a column, but it's something I had a lot of fun thinking about ... although I can't tell you why. Spoilers.

A writer toils away in obscurity, always on the edge of bankruptcy, then one day comes up with an idea that clicks: A child who suddenly enters an unknown world of magic and experiences danger and great adventure. The child is an orphan, but despite the doubts and fears of an unadventurous aunt and uncle, becomes a special person in this magical world.

The work becomes a phenomenon, spawning a series of best-selling, highly anticipated sequels, movies, toys, and even a theme park. Sure, some people complain about the magical world of witches, wizards, giants, and various monsters. Others are concerned with the way sometimes dark themes are matched with what some see only as children's stories. But overall parents enjoy the stories as much as their children, and the author becomes famous and generally loved until, sadly, he dies at an early age.

What? Who did you think I was talking about?

I'm speaking of L. Frank Baum, the author of fourteen Oz books – you've no doubt heard of the first one, *The Wonderful Wizard of Oz*.

The parallels between Baum and J.K. Rowling are obvious, and you can be forgiven for thinking I referred to the latter – after all, Harry Potter arrived on scene almost a century after Dorothy Gale was first carried to Oz, and many people have no idea her first appearance wasn't 39 years later, with the Judy Garland film version (which was far from the first Oz movie.)

Despite his health problems Baum was a writer of almost Bradbury-like proportions, churning out books and short stories (including some science fiction) under dozens of pennames. His third Oz book, in addition to bringing Dorothy back to Oz for the second time, introduced Tik-Tok, the mechanical man – one of the first robots ever in literature.

That makes Baum a pioneer of both American fantasy and the SF genre, not to mention a pioneer in film making: After becoming successful he moved to a tiny, almost empty village in an orange grove called Hollywood, and set up one of the area's first film studios.

What does this tell us?

As readers, it tells us we should always be searching for something new, even if it seems at first glance to be a "rip-off" of what we're already familiar with.

It tells writers something similar: There may be no new ideas, but there are always new ways to deal with old ideas. Despite their surface similarities, Rowling didn't steal from Baum; she just took similar concepts and made them her own. The Harry Potter books didn't lesson Baum's legacy – if anything, they complement each other.

I think Harry and Dorothy would have gotten along fine.

THE OZ MUSEUM, AND WHY YOU CAN'T GO THERE

This column is one of my greatest failures. Why? Because I wrote it clear back in the early 2000's, put it in storage along with several photos of the subject, and totally forgot about it.

By the time I found it again, it was too late to give this particular Oz museum a shout-out ... they had already closed. Sure, I made changes to account for that, but I still feel oddly responsible. Even more so now, when I double checked their online store and found that it, too, seems to have gone away. If I was the Tim Man, my tears would have rusted my jaws shut.

One of my earliest memories was reading the Oz books that my parents bought for me in the late 60's. The first of L. Frank Baum's fourteen Oz books has been the basis of several movies, the most famous of those starring Judy Garland: "The Wizard of Oz".

The movie was an annual TV tradition when I was a kid, but I didn't know anyone who'd even heard of the other books, let alone read them. Only in my teens did I learn there were more Oz books – more than 40 official ones, and many more unofficial trips to Oz, written after the originals went into the public domain. Years later I discovered I wasn't the only one harboring a love of Oz, and that there was an Indiana connection: The Yellow Brick Road Gift Shop and Oz Fantasy Museum in Chesterton.

(I'm told Baum, who lived in Chicago for awhile before leaving to form a movie company in a little California burg called Hollywood, had a summer home near Chesterton.)

I've had the pleasure of visiting three times, and finally got around to preparing this article, in which I was going to sing the praises of the little business on State Route 49 and encourage everyone to visit.

It was then that I discovered the Museum and storefront had closed at the end of 2008.

Don't get me wrong, the store still exists. But, like many other shops, it has become an online store now, specializing in Wizard of Oz related collectibles. That's allowed them to expand and update their business, and they can be found at ...

(Mark's note: I didn't print the link, because when I assembled this book the URL was for sale, but by the time you read this it might lead to some Munchkin-themed porn site.)

I'll certainly shop there, (*well, I would have. *sob*) but to me it's just not the same. There aren't a lot of places I can go to surround myself with Oz – in fact, that was it, within easy traveling distance. I was the proverbial boy in a candy shop whenever I stopped by, and I'm glad I got to visit one last time before they shuttered the doors. Sadly, the nearby Wizard of Oz Festival has also been canceled for 2009, a discovery I made right after telling some internet friends about it.

There's hope of a new festival being revived in Chesterton, and who knows? Maybe we'll all get a chance to visit again someday. Until then, all I can do is reminisce about the shop and museum.

It was 1973 – I was eleven years old – when Jean Nelson decided to sell dolls and dollhouse furniture in Chesterton. She named her shop The Yellow Brick Road after dreaming one night about the Wicked Witch of the West. It was just a fun name, at first – but then people started showing up to ask if there were Oz related items to be had. Apparently I wasn't the only one craving more Oz.

In 1980 an elderly lady walked into the shop, having come to visit it and Chesterton. The lady, Margaret Hamilton – you know her as the movie's Wicked Witch – suggested that Jean open an Oz museum. Well, you don't say no to the Wicked Witch!

That led to the first Wizard of Oz Festival in 1982, a small affair that soon ballooned into a three day event attracting up to 100,000 people. Ideas do tend to grow, don't they? Celebrities came too, among them many of those who played Munchkins in the movie.

That's the short version, believe me; a lot of Munchkins have marched down the yellow brick road since then, along with a change of ownership and the normal ups and downs of any small business. I don't know what the status of the location itself is, now that they've gone strictly online, but I hope it still looks as it did when I last visited.

There were the life-sized figures of the movie characters outside, along with Dorothy's house and other decorations. Inside is the store, which featured books, cards, figurines, clocks, trading cards, stickers, dolls, Dorothy costumes, games, mugs – let me take a breath – jewelry, lunch boxes, magnets, plates, posters, purses, signs, the odd ruby slipper .... and probably a lot more now, when they can turn their shopping area into inventory storage.

I bought an original Oz novel last time I was there, something that's stirred in me the urge that I first had back when I was a little kid: to write my own Oz story, someday. Why not? Baum's original characters are in the public domain, and rumor has it I'm a writer.

The museum was one room in the small shop, and to those used to big city museums it probably looked pathetic; but on closer examination, it was stuffed to the gills with things that, in some cases, can't be found anywhere else. That includes autographed items, rare toys, and figures commissioned exclusively for the store. I don't know what's happened to the collection, but I'm sending a copy of this article to the shop, so I'll keep you updated. *(Sob!)*

If I had any complaint about the shop and museum, it's that the place was movie centric and didn't have much book related material (Dorothy is blonde, doggone it!). But that's reality for you – as huge as the books were in the early part of the 20th century, they were eclipsed the moment Judy Garland started singing "Over the Rainbow". Maybe, someday, the books will come back into the imagination of today's children.

And who knows? When that happens, maybe Chesterton's celebration of Oz will rise again.

INTERSTITIAL SIX

MY HOUSE WANTS TO KILL ME

I think by now we all know that my house is trying to kill me.

It's my own fault. When I bought the thing it was already old and crotchety, and I haven't treated it well in the intervening years.

For instance, a couple of years ago one of the garage door springs broke. I discovered the door would go up and down just fine with only one spring, so I did what any broke and talentless maintenance hack would do: I ignored it. I mean, it still worked, right?

Then, late one summer, I reached up to pull the garage door down, and the other spring broke.

And the garage door pulled *me* down.

Many people get a rush out of going faster than a human being should go. From fighter pilots to roller coaster riders, we get a kick out of that uncontrolled feeling, that extreme speed. However, this only works when we know it's coming. I didn't.

I had my hand wrapped around the garage door handle when it suddenly changed from a door to an iron anvil that, in the best Wiley E. Coyote tradition, hurled toward the earth at three times the

147

speed of sound. It took my hand with it. My hand took my body with it.

At the base of that door is a concrete pad. The word "pad" is somewhat ironic, in this case.

I got slammed into the concrete like a pro wrestler at the losing end of the night's script.

It took a while for me to figure out exactly what happened. Well, it took a while for me to figure out *anything*. When I did, with the realization that I had neither the money nor the talent to fix the door, I decided this would be an excellent year to just park the car outside. On a related note, it wouldn't hurt to stop mowing a little early this season too, considering the mower was inside the garage, and the only door out was up a set of stairs and down another set.

(Naturally, it turned out to be a particularly cold and icy winter.)

So I got a lot of relaxation that fall. And by that, I mean I took hot Epsom salt baths while on heavy pain medications.

My garage, formerly a carriage house, in better days. Seriously, this was better days.

PART SEVEN:

politics
or:
maybe you shouldn't read this
section (my editor didn't)

If I'm anything, I'm libertarian. As a result, I hate pretty much everything having to do with the current federal government, but at least it gives humorists something to write about. Well, it gives all of us something to write about ... the difference is, I try not to let politics destroy my blood pressure level. Sometimes I even succeed. If you love anyone connected to our current government, or hate politics, or have high blood pressure, you might be better off skipping to Part 8.

POLITICS: A NIGHTMARE, BUT I REPEAT MYSELF

President Obama raised his eyebrow when Joe Biden walked into the Oval Office. His secretary had strict instructions to tell Biden that he was out of town. Always.

"Excuse me, Barrack – ah, Mr. President. We just got word that five men were caught breaking into the Republican National Committee headquarters."

"Oh, that's too bad." Obama didn't think it was all that bad, but on the other hand it wasn't a good idea to let people go around breaking into political offices.

"It gets worse. The FBI has connected cash found on the burglars to a slush fund – the Committee for the Reelection of President Obama slush fund."

"*What?*"

Biden looked embarrassed and a little confused. In fairness, he always looked confused. "Honestly, I thought we'd emptied out that fund during the third semi-monthly golf trip and weenie roast."

"But they can't connect that to me, can they? I didn't know about any break-in."

"Well, the good news is that you record all your conversations in the White House, which will prove that you didn't know about the break-in."

"Oh, good." Something nibbled at Obama's subconscious. Since when did he record his White House conversations? The NSA had assured him he had the only phone in the country that wasn't recorded.

"The bad news is that there's a suspicious 18 ½ minute gap in which the recordings have been erased by your secretary."

"Wait – what?'

"Between that and the admissions on other tapes that you're involved in the cover-up, you're bound to be impeached, or forced to resign." Biden crossed his arms and smiled. "And that makes me President."

That's when Barrack Obama woke up screaming.

After the Secret Service made sure there was nothing under the bed or in the closets, Obama told his wife, Michelle, about the dream. "It was terrible. It was as if I was ugly and un-charming like Nixon, but still stuck with Biden as my VP."

"Now, dear, just think of it this way: You have absolutely no scandal as bad as a burglary of the RNC headquarters."

"That's true."

"I mean, Benghazi happened clear over on the other side of the world, and you slept through the whole thing. Most people are still convinced it's about that silly video, and hardly anyone even remembers they asked for more security before those four people were killed."

"Yes, that's ... encouraging."

"And remember Fast and Furious? Here you are, a President trying to push through more and more gun control while your Department of Justice actually handed out illegal guns that were used to kill Mexicans and an American border guard. And yet for all that, our minions in the press have mostly managed to suppress the story."

"Yeah, well – plausible deniability, there."

"Absolutely, dear. I'll send the Secret Service down for some warm milk, while you consider the fact that we absolutely knew nothing about the IRS targeting conservative groups. We didn't, did we?"

"Hey, every administration does that!"

"Exactly, and that makes it okay. And those Associated Press telephone records that we seized? National security, baby."

"Right, and how can our friends in the press really complain, anyway? I mean, they practically elected me."

"Then there's that EPA stuff."

Obama choked on his warm milk. "EPA stuff? What EPA stuff?"

"Well, they gave taxpayer money to private green companies, even knowing the companies were financially unsound. Then they delayed the permit process for oil, coal, and natural gas companies. And it turns out the EPA director was using a fake e-mail account to hide official correspondence that should have been legally public. Other than that, not much."

Obama reached for the aspirin.

Michelle was on a roll. "Then there's all the data mining by the NSA –"

"Hey, Bush started that! He probably started all that stuff. Note to self: Check to see if Bush started all that stuff."

"That's true, dear, and if someone else did it before you, that means it's okay for you to do it, too."

The President glared at his wife, who was now counting off on her fingers.

"Then there's for Affordable Care Act, which few people are actually calling a scandal even though it's going to cost hugely more than was advertised. I suppose the scandal part could be how we say it's fair health care for everyone, but tried to give exemptions to elected officials –"

"Now, wait a minute, dear. I worked hard on that legislation, so hard that we had to get it passed so we could read it. Who could possibly be better at taking over medical and insurance decisions than the federal government?"

"You're absolutely right, dear. Besides, at least you've never had an affair while in the White House." Suddenly Michelle's expression turned ugly. "Have you?"

"No, ma'am."

"Oh, that's good. Because otherwise, you wouldn't be able to wake up every morning next to – this." Suddenly Michelle peeled her face back, to reveal the beady eyes and ski nose of Richard Nixon. "Now, don't worry: We are not a crook!"

That's when Obama woke up screaming again.

DENIAL IS A VIRUS IN EGYPT

This is an older column, but when I stumbled across it, I realized it was interesting in light of the current fuss about the Ebola virus. Ebola is one of those things I would not write a column about, what with people dying and stuff. Why is it in the politics section? Partially because this kind of medical event has been politicized, more and more. Mostly because I (thankfully) don't have many politics-related columns here, so I needed filler.

West Nile Virus is a serious disease, with the potential not only to harm humans, but also to devastate bird and livestock populations. We all wish it had stayed where it came from, which I can only assume would be somewhere west of the Nile, so you may be shocked to hear me say this:

We're taking it way too seriously.

What is it? A virus, thus the name. Who does it kill? The very old, very young, and already weak—it's the Hitler of diseases.

What are the symptoms? Aches, pains, high fever ...

Hey, wait a minute.

It's the flu, people.

Sure, it's an unusual flu, in light of the fact that we get it from mosquitos instead of each other, but that's actually good. Nobody wants to be around mosquitos, anyway.

Can you believe there's actually debate over spraying mosquitos? Are they kidding? Some people, possibly from the Society to Prevent Cruelty to Blood Sucking Insects, think we should save our disease-laden little friends. (Okay, they actually want to save the environment, but that would ruin the joke.)

I say, kill 'em all. The mosquitos, not the bleeding hearts. They're the terrorists of the bug world. Don't wait for a UN resolution, now that the bugs have developed a WMD of their own.

Apparently humans are a dead end for that virus, which sounds really bad but actually means we can get it, but not spread it around. Again, that's actually good. You can put a whole room full of West Wheezes, Nile Noses, and Virus—um—Vexes together, and they couldn't infect one other person. It's terrible that animal populations are suffering, but West Nile will be much less serious in the long run than, say, venereal disease. If you get that from wildlife, you've got bigger problems.

The numbers do disturb me a little. For instance, one expert insists this is a minor problem, in that only one person in a hundred is likely to get bitten by a mosquito carrying West Nile.

Pardon my math, but doesn't that make for about four hundred sick people just in Noble County?

But most who catch it will get no more sick than they would from the same flu we've been sharing for centuries, and those who are in trouble are the same ones endangered by Flu Classic. In 1917-

18 Flu Classic killed millions of people, and there wasn't a single mosquito involved.

You wouldn't know that to watch the news:

"Officials say you should stay home with all your doors and windows closed, locked, and bolted. Hide under your mattress, in a closet, while clutching a can of Raid. If you *must* go out, spray each member of your family with a full can of OFF, make sure you're covered head to toe with at least three layers of DDT-impregnated wool and leather, and set fire to any vegetation in your way. If you're bitten by a mosquito that's even seen photos of the Nile River, you WILL DIE."

But there are other viruses more dangerous than West Nile:

The Two-Beer Virus, which make people believe they're the best driver in the world, and indestructible. (So named because they always tell the police they've had "just two beers".)

The Mis-Dial virus, which makes people dial the wrong number, then be rude to whoever answers—as if the callee was responsible.

The Crest Vile Virus, which happens when people don't brush their teeth in the morning. Oddly, only the victims don't notice.

The Pest Dialed Virus, which you can avoid by signing up on the No Call Telemarketing list.

And of course, the West Noble Virus, which I only put in here because it's the name of a local school and I liked the play on words.

Any of these—with the exception of the last—may cause more trouble than West Nile, and don't involve insects unless "insects" is a metaphor for certain humans.

Meanwhile, has it occurred to anyone that all of Indiana will soon be inoculated by one big event that will, at least for awhile, remove the threat of mosquitoes completely?

It's called winter.

It would be ironic, though, if we emptied so many bug spray cans into the atmosphere that global warming kicked in, and the temperature didn't drop enough to kill insects. I'm up for that. I'll trade a few days in bed with a thermometer at 100 degrees for not seeing snow.

I have a feeling others won't agree.

THROWING GREEN AT GREEN

"Excuse me, President Obama? We have a problem."

There will be no problems in this administration, young man; only hope and change.

"Yessir, but ... it seems the Solyndra Company has filed for bankruptcy."

What? That's impossible. They can't fail – it's green energy! Green energy is our future, plus it's really cool. It's green, darn it!

"Apparently they couldn't compete with Chinese manufacturers of more conventional solar modules."

But didn't we give them a few million dollars?

"Um, half a billion. And the state of California gave them twenty-five million, give or take a hundred thousand."

Okay, well, just send them some more. What are printing presses for, if you can't print money with them?

"It's too late, Mr. President. All the employees were laid off without accrued vacation pay or benefits, and all the Solyndra executives took off with their five figure quarterly bonuses."

Why, that's horrible. *Horrible*, especially in these times of all-Bush's-fault high unemployment.

Those people involved should be punished severely, drawn and quartered, hung from the highest, thingamajig the Navy hangs people from – do we know their names?

"Oh, yes sir. Well, there's Executive V.P. of operations and engineering, Ben Bierman, V.P. of marketing Karen Alter, stakeholder George Kaiser –"

Wait – aren't those people who raised money for my election?

"Yes, why?"

Well, I'm sure they acted in good faith and did their very best ... why don't we cut them a break, and restructure the loan so that when the company is liquidated investors get paid before our loan is?

"But, sir – that's a half billion dollars in taxpayer money –!"

Printing presses, my friend. Besides, poor George Kaiser is a billionaire, so isn't he getting enough stress from our good Occupy friends without having to worry about where his next mansion comes from?

"But what will the press say about this?"

Tell them that if this blows up a Republican might get elected in 2012. That'll quiet down everyone who isn't Fox.

"But didn't you say transparency would be the hallmark of your administration?"

That's exactly right: I want everyone to be transparent. Everyone else. That way I know what they're up to. Let's not get silly with it, though.

"Mr. President, some people are already calling this crony capitalism –"

Now, everybody knows I don't like capitalism. Why risk the ups and downs of free enterprise when we can just let the government take care of anyone? Aren't people in countries with complete social and economic equality much happier?

"I'll ask the communists and get back to you, sir. But I was referring to *your* cronies."

Oh. Well, again, let's not get silly. Look, I don't understand this. We supported Solyndra, so they can't possibly fail. Just throw some more money at it. Couldn't we refinance their loan?

"We already did, sir, to the tune of an extra $67 million, but they still went bankrupt ... even after spending a million of it lobbying in Washington."

That just doesn't make any sense. The government's never wrong. I mean, not since 2008. I don't regret giving them the loan. It was a good bet, and they're green energy, and how can green energy be in the red?

"Can't argue with that, sir, what with you paying me and all, but here's a thought: What about trying true free enterprise?"

I don't understand.

"You know: No crony capitalism or corporate welfare, no risking taxpayer money in private business, no special interest preferences or tax breaks, no taxpayer funded bailouts. Free enterprise."

I ... you're not making any sense. How would that work?

"Well, the government would step out of the way of entrepreneurs and inventors, small business people and job creators. As long as they worked within the law and competed fairly with each other they'd be allowed to sink or swim according to the laws of supply and demand. You know – the way America became great to begin with."

Are you insane? How can we control that?

"We're not supposed to control the people, Mr. President; they're supposed to control us."

Who came up with that idea? We made another billion dollars in loans to green companies; are you telling me we should just let the people choose what they do and don't buy, and what companies they do and don't support? Next thing you'll be telling me is that we should tell everyone what we knew about Solyndra's failure. What's next? Writing laws the average person can understand? Making Congress and the President abide by the same rules as everyone else?

"What was I thinking, sir?"

Look, you let me think for the people. You just do what I pay you for: Go out and find out a way to

show this is all Bush's fault. And hurry, I've got a
fund raiser tomorrow.

HOWIE DUNNIT TAKES THE HEAT

I've written about Howie many times. He's a real person ... in my head.

"I want to talk to you about illegal immigration," said my friend Howie Dunnit, as I cowered behind the overgrown shrubs by my front porch. The reason Howie is my friend is because he's very good at sneaking up on me.

No way, Howie, I said.

"But I've studied up on the issue. I actually read stuff, and things."

Oh, *really?*

"Yeah, I studied it objectively for half an hour."

Well, that puts you ahead of most people. (I was impressed that Howie managed to insert a four syllable word into a sentence. Still, he can be insightful, in an idiot savant kind of way.)

"The way I see it, we're all illegal immigrants except the Indians, and even they came to this country at one time, from India or something."

Oh, well done, Howie.

"We can claim this country, even though we didn't go through the turnstile and fill out the paperwork, because we beat the Indians. So if the current crop of illegal immigrants wants to be able to stay here legally, all they really have to do is kill all our cows and give us smallpox."

That – ah – hm...

"Let me check my notecard, here ... in 1900, there were about a million illegal Mexican immigrants in the US, not including people from other places, like Georgia and Georgia."

Howie, one Georgia is –

"Forget it, I'm on a roll. So in 1986 the Feds legalized illegal immigrants who got here before 1982, and about three million got legal status. The idea was that we'd then tighten up border security, just like most countries do, and the illegal immigration problem would be over."

I guess –

"And now we have eleven million illegal immigrants."

Well, yeah, but this time the government has promised to actually address the problem of border security.

Howie just looked at me.

Okay, that does ring just a bit hollow ...

"Maybe I'm being Mr. Obvious, but if the laws were enforced from the get-go, we wouldn't have this problem."

You *are* being Mr. Obvious.

"But everyone wants to turn it into a race thing. Let me ask you this: Why are most illegal immigrants Hispanic?"

Because we border Mexico?

"Nice, you get a cookie. Now, would people look at the whole thing differently if the problem was coming from Canada?"

But Mexico has a horrible economy, rampant crime, a corrupt government, severe weather coming in from both sides –

"As opposed to here."

But Canada's just ... nice. Except for the weather, and at least they don't get hurricanes from both directions. Very friendly –

"You're missing my point. Put Canada in Mexico. Canada's being taken over by drug gangs, Canada's government is useless, Canada's economy crashed. Now, how would you feel about a flood of illegal immigrants from Canada?"

Well, I'd feel the same. What difference does it make what country they're coming from? If we bordered Australia I'd say the same thing.

"Good, now approach it from that angle – takes all the race right out of it. I've got a quiz for you."

Please, no ...

"First, why do legal immigrants support illegal immigration?"

What? Why wouldn't they?

"Because nobody likes a line jumper. Here are people who jumped through hoops, waited years so they could become Americans, then somebody sneaks across the border and gets legal status with the stroke of a pen? And making all of them look bad. Legal immigrants should be leading the charge to secure the border."

That makes sense. Did I just say that?

"Second, what do all illegal immigrants, no matter what country, have in common?"

Um ... fake social security cards?

"Here's a hint: They're all here *illegally*."

That's a pretty big hint.

"Realistically, should a large number of people be rewarded for doing something illegal, just because there are a lot of them? Then why shouldn't we pull over speeders and give them candy?"

I think the free candy budget is covered under Obamacare.

"Third: How many potential terrorists have crossed into the US from the south?"

A lot less than drug dealers. You can get some really good stuff from over the border. I've heard.

"7,518 illegal aliens caught, coming from countries labeled as state sponsors of terrorism. In one year. I memorized that one, proud of me?"

The word is amazed.

"Fourth, how much would it cost to secure the US-Mexico border?"

About 22.4 billion dollars just to build one fence.

"Hey, you got that one!"

I can't let you beat me, Howie. The President burns up that much cash just on golfing trips.

"What? Really?"

We'll discuss the comedic technique of over exaggeration later.

"Whatever. Fifth: How much does it cost to take care of illegal immigrants?"

About a hundred billion a year, for the federal and state governments. But immigrants contribute, too.

"Yeah, they do, which brings me to question Six: Would it be better for them to contribute as legal residents?"

Um ... yes?

"Good, that was a softball. Seven: What would happen if an American crossed illegally into almost any other country in the world?"

Um ... some form of arrest and deportation?

"Very good, I think you're up to a D+."

Yay! Just like in chemistry class!

"Now that we've established illegal immigration is illegal, and should be treated as an illegal act instead of some race-baiting political bull, what should we do about it?"

You're asking me?

"I only studied this for half an hour."

Oh. Well, we could streamline the legal immigration process, then put all illegal immigrants back into the line and have them go through the process to be here legally, so they can contribute and so their first act as Americans isn't committing a crime.

"Hey, you pass! Bonus question: Why will this never happen?"

Um ... because nobody in Washington can tackle any common sense question without turning it into a big political war?

"You get an A for effort. And they get an F."

PROGNOSTICATION IS ALSO MY MIDDLE NAME

(Author's note: I wrote this years ago, before the Great Recession, before curiously timed election year Foley revelations, and before a surprisingly strong group of economic indicators. I originally wrote: "Neither (Foley and economic indicators— look them up) sways my predictions, which I wrote in one sitting while doped up on cold medicine. Although I did believe about half these would actually happen – you judge which half – I strongly suggested no one bet money on it.)

Like most prognosticators, I usually reserve my predictions column until the end of the year. But I don't see any point in waiting because, frankly, I'm usually wrong.

I sure hope I'm wrong this time.

I say that because we're in for a recession, most likely a worldwide one, the worst since the early 1980's. I can't tell you exactly when it will start, but batten down the hatches, 'cause it's coming.

One big indicator of an economic downturn is when automakers start tightening their belts. As usual, America's automakers were far behind the times, continuing to turn out big ol' SUV's when the high gas price writing was on the "holy cow! We can't afford this" wall. There may be a rally in the used car market, as people trade for cars that could fit in the trunks of their old vehicles, but the gas-sucking gravy train is over. Where the consumers go, the automakers go. Where the automakers go, the parts suppliers go. Where the parts suppliers go – well, we're all going to heck in a hand basket, misery loves company, and all sorts of other clichés to substitute for "Here comes trouble".

Meanwhile, back at the ranch house, the housing boom bubble is bursting as we speak. A lot of people have been making their living in the construction industry, but, like an overdose of Ex-Lax, it's an artificial movement that can't be sustained forever.

Add the two together, and the economy is going to dump like ... well, see above about Ex-Lax. That's one reason why I'm making my predictions now: I have an uneasy feeling all this will be obvious by early next year.

Here's how the rest of the decade and beyond will go:

November, 2006: The Democrats take control of both houses of Congress in not-very-close elections. For the next two years G.W. Bush uses his veto power more than in the entire previous six years of his presidency. Except for the ongoing attempts to impeach Bush, the government grinds to a halt. No one notices.

Attempts are made by Congress to impeach every future president until 2042, when President Jenna Bush successfully pushes through an amendment to the Constitution that punishes "frivolous impeachment" with large fines.

February, 2007: Riots break out in several Wal-Marts when employees begin putting up Christmas, 2007 merchandise displays.

May, 2007: The 2008 presidential campaign begins in earnest. By the end of the year there are 26 Democrat candidates, 19 Republican candidates, 78 independent candidates, and Ralph Nader.

August, 2007: Ford declares bankruptcy, beginning a long legal battle that culminates in a government bail-out. By 2011 Ford is solvent again, and making a profit off hybrid electric cars they've had the technology for since 1989.

November, 2007: Rumors circulate that Fidel Castro is dead -- again. In 2012 Cuban authorities finally admit Castro died in 1987, and they've been circulating old footage of him ever since.

In 2013, Castro's 26 year old clone takes control of Cuba.

Spring, 2008: As the primary season begins, the mainstream media makes a concentrated effort to uncover every single bad thing every Republican candidate ever did. Fighting back, bloggers and Midwest talk show hosts begin a similar investigation of all Democratic candidates.

In response, by July, 2008, *all* presidential candidates drop out of the race. Ralph Nader declares himself provisional leader and attempts to move into the White House, but is driven off by a cigar-wielding Rush Limbaugh. A grass roots campaign to draft Colin Powell begins, but he flees the country.

August, 2008: Terrorists attack a major American city, killing several dozen people and injuring thousands in the hopes of controlling the election results. (*Mark's note: I have no memory of why I suddenly turned dark with this one.*)

September, 2008: After three days of waving banners and screaming, Republicans pick a far right wing conservative, and the Democrats a far left wing liberal for their Presidential candidates. Both claim to represent the "common" people.

November, 2008: Moderate voters stay away from the polls in droves, but of the 15% who do vote, a small majority vote for the Democratic candidate. The Democrats declare they've been given a mandate by America to make changes, which they proceed to not make. Colin Powel returns from his "vacation" in Australia.

Early 2009: Bio-fuels have become so successful in North America that foreign oil imports actually fall. Certain countries get *very* nervous.

October, 2010: The Cubs lose the World Series when a playback review reveals their winning runner forgot to touch third base.

November, 2010: Republicans make gains in the mid-term elections, but Democrats retain control of the House and Senate.

Summer, 2011: The recovering economy takes a hit when bad weather across the country ruins crops. For the first time, people wonder what will happen if all that bio-fuel has to go back to making food.

September, 2011: New Orleans sinks. Ex-mayor Nagin stages a protest in front of ex-President Bush's ranch.

January, 2012: Food riots break out – there's enough to supply everyone, but not enough bio-diesel to get the food to market.

May, 2012: Astronomers continue arguing over whether Pluto is a planet.

November, 2012: The President is reelected in a squeaker, thanks in part to the first Hispanic Vice-Presidential candidate. Recounts are necessary in Pennsylvania, New Jersey, and the new state of West Michigan.

March, 2013: A comet wipes out New Jersey. The parties blame each other. Mayor Nagin, recently relocated to Hoboken, claims NASA steered the asteroid there to wipe out the African-American population. Jesse Jackson leads a march.

July, 2014: The first coal fueled, steam powered car goes online. Everyone proclaims it the most original thing they've ever seen.

Print this out, people. Wait and see.

THERE'S A FINE LINE BETWEEN "HISTORY BUFF" AND "OLD GUY TELLING STORIES"

While finishing up this book, I was put into contact with a national publishing company that was considering a book about the history of Albion, Indiana. This is my home town, where I've lived for so long that I can remember not having cable TV or having to put in area codes.

I've lived here for so long that I've ridden on all but one of every gasoline powered fire engine Albion has ever had—and they got their first one in 1929.

I've lived here for so long that I know what people mean when they mention the "Halfway Pavement" ... even though that road's been fully paved since before I was born.

None of this information is particularly useful. The really useful thing about knowing history is that you can avoid repeating it, so I do my best not to move to a place that doesn't have cable, not to go to an emergency in a fire engine with no roof, and not to live on a gravel road. I guess it *is* useful.

I contracted with Arcadia Publishing, and after August, 2015 you should be able to buy *Images of America: Albion and Noble County*. The publisher threw me off when they decided to encompass all of

Noble County, but what the heck—if you're an Albion native, you're pretty much automatically a Noble County native. How hard could it be?

It was hard. It was hard because I'm a writer, and *Images of America* books are about—wait for it—images. For reasons I won't go into here, we had a tough time getting all the historical photos around in time to make the deadline, but my wife pulled a couple of marathon organizing sessions and we were in business.

Here's the weird part: I now love local history.

Am I getting old?

As a kid the only history I was interested in was that involving warfare, which is fairly common with young kids who haven't been exposed to the realities of warfare. As an adult, I figured out that I had a responsibility to follow politics and current affairs, and you can't really understand that stuff without understanding history, so I started studying national and world history despite myself.

Then I wrote a book about the history of my local fire department, because as a volunteer firefighter I loved firefighting and old fire trucks. Next thing I knew, I had a love for local history.

Yeah, I'm one of those people.

For the newest book, I studied when buildings were built, burned, and rebuilt, why this piece of ground is flat and that one has a kettle lake, who begat who and how they're related to the other who. I learned fascinating, surprising, and sometimes stunning things.

Well ...

Fascinating, surprising, and sometimes stunning if you're into that kind of stuff. Yes, I spent hours going over old postcards with a magnifying glass, and trying to figure out why a guy moved his blacksmith shop two blocks, and where the heck Hawpatch was. It was ... well, fascinating.

If you're into that kind of stuff.

If you're not, let's be frank, it's boring.

Oh, I'll defend it. I'll defend my interest all day long, because you have to know where you're coming to know where you're going. Also, because few people today truly realize how difficult life was for the people who ultimately birthed our towns and cities. (Not literally ... sheesh.) Also because, doggone it, it's actually interesting once you pay attention.

But, just in case, remember that I've written lots of stuff. Three romantic comedies, a young adult novel, a collection of short stories, and you've maybe heard of my humor writing. So I'm begging you: If I ever launch into a four hour long lecture of the Black family's role in growing Albion, or what A.J. Denlar went through before he became Albion's first fire chief ... if your eyes start glazing over and you get TMJ symptoms from yawning too hard ...

Just stop me.

I'll get over it.

Sure, I can tell you all about this building. Don't ask - just run.

PART EIGHT:

what's the sundry word for miscellaneous?

Historical coincidence, diets, holidays, college ... what do these things have in common?

Nothing.

But my next Slightly Off The Mark book, should there be one, will be much better organized per the previously mentioned most common column topics. Why? For the same reason I divided this disparate work into sections: Why not?

Oh—disparate! There's another word for miscellaneous!

WILLIAM MCLEAN'S FRONT PARLOR

I've never had a job that didn't feature some variation of the Checkout Syndrome, where everyone in the store heads to the checkout lanes at the same time. Now I take 911 calls for a living: You can go for an hour without a single call, then the phone rings ten times in two minutes.

"Yes, I understand you're on fire, but can you hold, please? This other guy fell in the river. Maybe I could introduce you."

Coincidences can be interesting. By coincidence, I found a list of weird coincidences at the very same time that I needed a subject to write about that wasn't politics or weather.

Let's start with flight, for instance, and Ohio. Orville and Wilbur Wright, who made the first powered airplane flight and were the first people to lose their luggage, were from Ohio.

Almost sixty years later, the US decided to put men into space, so naturally, they thought: Where can we find someone crazy enough to be the first ... oh, Ohio! And they found John Glenn.

Then they decided to land a man on the Moon. It was almost as dangerous as driving around Indianapolis, so they again looked to Ohio for crazy people, and found Neil Armstrong. That flight went okay ... in fact, the closest call the Moon missions had was when Apollo 13 experienced a catastrophic failure so major that Tom Hanks starred in a movie about it. Hanks played real life mission commander Jim Lovell ... of Ohio.

Twenty-two astronauts came from Ohio. Now, that's either coincidence, or people really want to get out of that state.

One of the turning points of World War II was the Battle of Midway. It didn't start out well for the US, though: the Japanese shot down every one of the first squadron of torpedo planes to attack their carriers, and the American dive bombers that were supposed to go in along with them got lost on the way.

Things looked bleak, until the commander of the dive bombers, which were almost out of fuel, spotted a Japanese ship and followed its path straight to his target.

The planes that were supposed to be guarding the Japanese carriers were busy shooting down the American torpedo planes. There were other planes on the Japanese ships, though: being rearmed for the next attack, and utterly unable to mount a defense.

By coincidence, the dive bombers arrived just when the Japanese carriers were most vulnerable, and by vulnerable I mean they're now resting on the bottom of the Pacific.

Wars are full of coincidences. Wars are also full of people who want to avoid wars. In 1861 Wilmer McLean happened to live along the road that went straight between Washington, D.C., and Richmond, Virginia. It was his bad luck that Richmond became the capital of the new Confederacy.

McLean happened to live in Manassas, Virginia, which also happened to be where the Union and Confederate armies met for the first time. In fact, Confederate General Beauregard picked McLean's house for his headquarters, which made it as a tempting target.

Sure enough the Union, in true *Star Wars* fashion, dropped a cannonball right down the house's chimney. No one inside was hurt and McLean stuck around, right until a year later when an even bigger clash – the *Second* Battle of Bull Run – broke out in his front yard.

McLean decided it might be a good time to choose a different home.

So he moved to Clover Hill, Virginia, nowhere near the route between the two capitals. Didn't help. In that town, by then renamed Appomattox Court House, General Grant accepted the surrender of Confederate General Lee.

In Wilmer McLean's front parlor.

Edgar Allan Poe released his only novel, *The Narrative of Arthur Gordon Pym of Nantucket*, in 1838. Poe, trying like all authors to push some copies out the door, claimed the book to be based on true events.

It told of the four surviving members of a wrecked sailing ship. The starving men draw lots, and the loser, a cabin boy named Richard Parker, becomes … dinner.

Well, Poe was that kind of writer.

Here's the coincidence: It turns out Poe was right, his book really did detail true events. The four survivors of a shipwreck did draw lots, and they did pick their cabin boy, Richard Parker, to later be, um, picked out of their teeth.

Oh, I forgot to mention: That wreck happened forty-six years *after* Poe wrote his novel.

Another novelist, the much more forgotten Morgan Robertson, wrote *Futility, or the Wreck of the Titan*. It was about a massive ocean liner, the largest ship afloat and "unsinkable". A British steel vessel, it was about 800 feet long and sank after hitting an iceberg in the North Atlantic, at about midnight in April.

You have to wonder why nobody sued Robertson, who other than making the ship's name slightly different was clearly telling the story of the *Titanic*. He even had the ship meet its fate at the exact location the real one did, while traveling at close to the same speed. The lack of lifeboats for all the passengers was mentioned, and the point of impact was the same.

If you've been paying attention at all so far, you may have guessed the connection between this and Poe's story. Robertson wrote his book in 1898. The *Titanic* sank fourteen years *later*.

Finally, here's my favorite coincidence:

Three of the first five US Presidents died on July 4th – Independence Day. That's also the date the Battle of Gettysburg was won, which also happens to be the same day General Grant captured Vicksburg,

Mississippi after a long Civil War campaign. But never mind that, here's the really fun part:

Just before John Adams died, on July 4th, 1826 – fifty years to the day after America's birth – he murmured, "Thomas Jefferson survives." He and Jefferson had become bitter political rivals, but in later years made up and became best buds.

Only Thomas Jefferson hadn't survived. He'd died hours before, also on America's fiftieth birthday. (Fifth President James Monroe died exactly five years later.)

Maybe it's just a coincidence.

WON'T YOU EAT CARBS, BILL BAILEY?

I have a healthy skepticism of any and all dietary plans and weight loss "experts". As I've mentioned before, my diet book would be so clear and simple that it would consist of only three pages:

1. Eat less.

2. Exercise more.

3. Repeat.

In reality, I could then fill up the book with how to accomplish that fourth, all-important step: Have willpower. I haven't cracked that one, yet.

Although those steps will work, it's also true that you can tweak both diet and exercise in ways that help you lose weight faster. It's also true that losing weight alone doesn't make a person healthy: I give you as a famished example rail-thin, malnourished supermodels. At the beginning of last winter I was close to thirty pounds overweight (although I've somehow lost some since), and was *still* more healthy than any number of skinny people who I could snap like a twig.

Better to meet in the middle – or, for you vegans, to vegetate in the middle. That's all well and good, but who do you believe? Eat all protein; eat all veggies; eat nothing but cabbage soup. (I actually tried the cabbage soup diet, and did lose weight even though it was winter. Plus, fringe benefit, once it worked its way through my system nobody wanted to be around me.)

Now I've discovered a new twist, on a website I won't name because by now they're probably reversed their recommendations: Packing on the carbs.

Oh. Really?

What this article is talking about is Resistant Starch, which is what happens when your dry cleaner goes overboard with your suit and it won't bend to fit your body, and is also apparently a kind of food. Starches would be that stuff people are always telling me not to eat. Like baked potatoes. Yum ...

Resistant starches apparently include bananas and oatmeal, beans, potatoes, and plantains, which are like plantations only built under mountains. Also included is Pearl Barley, who you might know as a singer made immortal in the song, "Won't you come home, Pearl Barley?" Pearl Barley, as I recall, was a very large woman, which makes me question her diet and make me wonder if she didn't come home because she was at a fast food place.

(Oh my gosh – I just checked, and Pearl Bailey died twenty years ago! Is part of getting older having to explain your jokes to younger people? Also, it was her brother, Bill Bailey, who didn't come home – possibly because she sent him for takeout.)

(Bill isn't really Pearl's brother ... I think.)

But according to this article, which is written with all the authority of someone with a website of their very own, resistant starches are cool, which makes them hot. The reasons:

1. Carbs fill you up.

That makes them appetite suppressants, more filling than protein or fat and supposedly digested more slowly. I usually accomplish the same goal of losing my appetite by watching disgusting TV shows: The Bachelor, Dirty Jobs, or ... well, with Olbermann gone from MSNBC, I might have to try the baked potatoes.

2. Carbs curb your hunger.

Researchers say that when dieters go from a low-carb diet to one high in fiber and resistant starches, their cravings go to the curb.

Not unless they make resistant starch chocolate bars, bub.

3. Carbs control blood sugar and diabetes.

One study indicated a 38% improvement in blood sugar and insulin response, if carbs were eaten in certain combinations. Which is actually an idea I can't make much fun of.

4. Carbs speed up metabolism.

In other words, the body fires up its natural fat burners. Usually, when I burn fat, I have to run for a fire extinguisher. In this case the body releases fatty acids, which sounds disgusting but kicks your metabolism right in its overly padded butt.

5. Carbs make you lose belly fat faster than other foods.

Even when the same number of calories is consumed this is true – calories, keep in mind, are a unit of measurement, so in theory one calorie is the same as another. In actual practice, with carbs the calories are the same, but the body burns them faster. Imagine the federal government maintaining the same income but decreasing spending. No, seriously, imagine it. Just try. Stop laughing.

6. Carbs keep you satisfied.

Foods high in resistant starch trigger your body's fullness signals. Your brain says, "Gee, I'm full – I don't want to eat anymore". You'll no longer crave foods, and can then go on to craving other stuff, like brains. Carbs will start the zombie apocalypse!

7. Carbs make you feel good about you.

That's because dieters can lose weight without doing something really unhealthy, such as cutting out food groups, crash dieting, or cutting off a limb. They feel empowered by the results, although be warned: You'll never be a runway supermodel.

The main problem I have with this article is that there's a dearth of sources quoted. Dearth is more than an evil Sith Lord, by the way. Is this a big study, or the result of a poll taken after a big family reunion?

I'll consider that one over dinner.

DO YOU WANT TO BUILD A ZOMBIE?

Apparently there's a rumor going around that 2014 had the first Halloween in 666 years to fall on Friday the Thirteenth.

gasp Extra shenanigans this time around! Instead of harmless pranks ... *pure evil*. And the next week an election, which these days is pretty much the same thing.

Okay, now let's put on our thinking caps and consider this for a moment, folks. Halloween ... on Friday the *Thirteenth* ... thinking ... thinking.

There you go.

For those of you who still haven't caught up, it's impossible for one simple reason: The modern Halloween, originally "All Hallows Eve", dates back only to the mid-16th century, so this couldn't be the 666th outing.

Didn't think about that, did you?

Besides, these days the number of the beast is ... what is the address for Congress, anyway? 666 Pennsylvania Avenue?

No, turns out it's East Capitol St NE & First ST SE, so the address is nowhere near as scary as the occupants. You'll never find a more wretched hive of scum and villainy, or at least that's what Obi-Wan Kenobi said. Or was it Joe Biden? One of them is from another galaxy, and the other's a Jedi.

Halloween does, indeed fall on a Friday this year, and less than a week before the truly frightening day from hell, which this year falls on November 4th.

I used to like Halloween. (I never liked elections.) Now my wife no longer lets me eat Halloween candy, just because of some ridiculousness about my doctor, and my impending death. How does he know, really? I might be better off getting a diagnosis from a meteorologist. But now I'm off candy, and the only thing left is short days, cold nights, and dead leaves.

So I rested my exhausted imagination and cheated, by searching around the internet for something original having to do with Halloween. I don't know why; I don't bother with originality the rest of the year.

Lists of the most popular Halloween costumes are common, as usual. For instance, sisters could dress up as Elsa and Anna from *Frozen*, since that's what they'll probably be anyway. They can walk down the street singing, "Do You Want to Build a Snowman", and if it's a typical Indiana Halloween, they might then be able to actually build one.

According to Party City—and isn't that somewhere we all want to be?—the Frozen characters are indeed one of the top ten Halloween trends of this year. I'd like to be the snowman, Olaf, from that movie, because I can picture dressing up in a white sheet, and stuffing it full of lots and lots of insulation. I'll be warm, or (since no one could tell it was me) I could take the next logical step and pay someone else to pretend to be me.

The next is a Minion, from that movie with Minions in it. You'd be all yellow and have one eye, and next year you could recycle the costume, add an extra eye, and go as one of "The Simpsons".

Honestly, I kind of lost interest after that, until I got to #5: "Geek Chic".

No. Geeks are not chic. That's the whole point, and I should know: I was one.

Zombies were on the list, with the danger that people might think you're just an early voter ... and in that case they might also think any vampire trailing you is just a politician.

Abandoning the party, I leaped over to Halloween Express, which should certainly know something on the subject. Sure enough, they had not one, but ten top 2014 costume lists.

There were, of course, the ones for kids, teens, and toddlers, as well as funny, sexy, and couples costumes.

There was also a list of costumes for pets. Honestly, I think that's cruel. They don't get why it's fun ... and they don't get candy.

There were also plus sized costumes. That does make sense, these days. But ... and I don't mean to offend ... plus sized Spider-Man?

Not as scary as the plus sized tooth fairy, but still.

Maybe I'll just go this year the way I do every year: As the driver ... in the car ... with the heater. Protecting the candy.

Oh, by the way, for those of you who didn't figure it out, Halloween doesn't fall on the 13th this year because it always falls on the 31st. April Fools!

WHY, KAPPA? WHY?

My ego really took a hit when I started living with someone smarter than me.

Remember those standardized tests we took in high school? Mine always came out average, right down the line. Reading comprehension? A little above average. Math? Well, something had to score low so it could average out. I would tell my guidance counselor that I wanted to get involved in entertainment or emergency services, and she'd steer me toward the stability of the service industry.

My wife is one of those people who got bored in school, because it was too easy. I know – hard to imagine, right? If a 4.0 grade point average is perfect, they had to set up a special 4.1 for her. (And why 4.0, anyway? Why not 100%, or at least 10? Guess I'm not smart enough to understand that.)

It came as no surprise to me when she got a letter from Phi Kappa Phi, inviting her to be a member of their organization. Let's face it, smart people are the main target of those groups with the Greek names. Or is it Latin? Or something otherworldly?

Naturally, I was ecstatic for Emily's sake. "This is great!" I told her. "Beer bongs! Wet t-shirt contests! People getting thrown through windows! You can have guests, right?"

The way our luck has been going, we'd both catch pneumonia at a wet t-shirt contest.

It turns out I was thinking of sororities, or fraternities, or paternities – or maybe that last one happens after sororities and fraternities. I got confused by all the Dead Language letters in the title. By the way, it's a bad idea to react to this invitation by looking at the title and saying, "Two thighs? Well, doesn't that kappa all."

Phi Kappa Phi—which has nothing to do with chicken, or sex of any form, and on a related note Emily's a really good shot with a thrown shoe—is, in fact, a collegiate honor society. I thought collegiate was something you put on your skin. Or is that Calgon?

It is, in fact, the oldest, largest, and most selective collegiate honor society for all academic disciplines in the entire country, and had chapters on more than 300 campuses. Only the top 10% of seniors are eligible.

I know what you're thinking: "What's academic discipline?" Well, it means you'd better work your butt off if you want to get in, that's what it means. The closest I ever came to academic discipline was once in elementary school, when I got paddled for not moving my blocks fast enough after playtime. (It was really for not paying attention – I didn't hear the teacher tell us to put them away – and not paying attention was my problem in school from then on.)

Anyway, Phi Kappa Phi was started in 1897 when a group of students at the University of Maine got together and said, "You know what? There is *nothing* to do up here. We're in the middle of nowhere, it's freaking freezing *all the time* ... what the heck, let's crack this book of Klingon phrases and see what we can do with it."

(I kid – while Latin and Greek are often considered dead languages, lots of humans speak Klingon. Ironic, much?)

Some famous Phi Kappa Phi members include:

Stephen Ambrose, who wrote some of my favorite historical books and was involved in two of the best World War II film projects ever, *Band of Brothers* and *Saving Private Ryan.*

Jimmy Carter, living proof that you can be both a bad President and a good man. (*Mark's note: In the time since I originally wrote this, my view of him has gone down a few points.*)

Hillary Clinton, who potentially found a way around the two term rule by serving eight years as the President during someone else's administration.

James Barksdale, who as president and CEO of Netscape Communications initiated many of us into the wonders of waiting on that dial-up sound.

Ruth Bader Ginsburg, second woman and first Jewish Supreme Court Justice.

John Grisham, who had produced some of the longest novels I've never been able to finish.

William Howard Taft, our fattest President ... hey, you take your fame where you can get it, and he was a big, big man.

Shlomo Sawilowsky, Rabbi and professor. No, I never heard of him until now – I just love his name.

Ferdinand Marcos, 10th President of the Philippines. Because every organization needs a dictator.

Phi Kappa Phi's motto is Philosophia Krateito Photon, and of course I'm not spelling those correctly, which helps explain why I'm not a member. Philosophia is a girl I used to date in high school; Krateito was one of Michael Jackson's older brothers and a member of the Jackson 5; and Photon is, of course, a type of torpedo used by the Klingons. See, I told you the Klingons were involved!

But seriously, it translates roughly to "Let the love of learning rule humanity". In the end, no matter how much smarter she is than I am, one thing Emily and I have in common is the love of learning.

So, now my baby gets the recognition she deserves for being a smart cookie. I wonder: What Phi Kappa Phi member will she walk in the footsteps of? Will she be a politician? (Oh, I hope not.) Astronaut? Or, more likely, writer? Or will she head straight for the dictator role?

With credentials like that, who would tell her no?

Thanks for stopping by, folks, and tell all your friends. If you don't have any, tell your enemies. And remember: If you get mediocre grades, skip higher education, break things a lot, develop no appreciable job skills, and hone a keen sense of irony, you too might someday become a successful humorist.

Well, a humorist, anyway.

Or, you could go to college ... or vocational school. I'm just saying, keep your options open.

I don't need the competition.

SNEAK PEEK:
MARK'S NEXT FICTION PROJECT

Everybody loves a bonus. I love bonus material on movie DVDs ... remember DVDs? You may like bonus little foam hearts on your overpriced spiced coffee. Instead, and just to show I can write something besides humor, I offer you as a bonus the first snippet of my upcoming novel: Beowulf: In Harm's Way.

You do already think I can write humor, right? I mean, you got this far ...

This is the story of a spaceship crew during an interstellar war, some five hundred years in the future. It would probably fit under the subgenre "space opera", and I tried to put a fun, humorous twist to the whole "The future of the galaxy is on the line and we could die horribly at any moment" thing. 'Cause what's more fun than violent conflict?

BEOWULF: IN HARM'S WAY

A red light flashed on the shuttle's control board.

Lieutenant Commander Paul Gage leaned forward, his hands still on the little craft's controls. "What did I do?"

Beside him, Kurt Biermann shook his head. "Nothing, Skipper—that's a comm alert from the bridge."

"Well, that's damned inconvenient when I'm trying to get certified as a shuttle pilot." Thank goodness they were parked in his ship's shuttle bay, running a simulation. Gage couldn't remember piloting anything since ... since the incident. Since the start of the war.

The real pilot chuckled. "You know, a ship's captain doesn't have to know how to fly a shuttle. Since I'm usually up at the *Beowulf's* helm, I'm the one who should be practicing down here."

"I ordered cross-training, so I cross-train." Gage punched the comm button. He'd ordered random drills, and it would be bad form if he didn't show up for battle stations. Second Lieutenant. Biermann, who no doubt hadn't expected to train anyone while running a shakedown cruise in a ship with only forty-two crewmembers, looked relieved.

"Damage control stations, all hands, we have a fire in engineering. This is not a drill."

While Gage punched the shuttle's door open and leaped out, he noticed Biermann no longer looked relieved. The young helmsman followed him through the shuttle bay airlock, turned toward the bridge, then looked surprised when Gage split from him at the main corridor.

As Gage ran toward engineering—the crew wasn't supposed to run, but he wasn't the only one squeezing through the narrow corridors at a sprint—he tapped his earbud. "Bridge from Gage, I'm heading directly to engineering. Who has the con?"

"Mr. Endo is on the bridge, sir."

"Very well." Sachiko Endo would tear her hair out at Gage breaking protocol by not going to the command center. Besides, that would leave her stuck on the bridge, and she always liked to be in the thick of things, but ... captain's privilege.

It didn't take long to approach the engineering area. It didn't take long to reach anywhere, on a ship the size of *Beowulf*. But before he could reach the last turn in the hallway he heard the muffled thump of running feet, and a quick, rasping breath.

A figure lumbered around the corner, completely encapsulated in silvery firefighting gear. Gage couldn't tell who it was: Fog covered the faceshield, and if Gage hadn't held his arm out the crewman would have rammed right into him.

Feeling an obstruction, the firefighter spun around, then began to flail when Gage grabbed him by the arm. "Stop there, crewman—this is the Captain."

"We're gonna blow up! The ship is gonna blow up!"

Gage disengaged the man's helmet shield and hauled it off, revealing a wild shock of black hair and wide eyes. "No, don't—we're all gonna die!" His voice was still muffled, coming through a breathing air mask.

Steadying the man with one arm, Gage pulled the mask forward as hard as he could, then let it snap back into place.

"Ow!"

He really didn't expect it to work, but the man stopped long enough to peel off the mask. He was trying to shake off the pain when Gage got into his face.

"You have an action station, Specialist Delacort."

With a trembling breath, Delacort tried to control himself. He didn't succeed very well. "Sir, there's a fire in the FTL drive."

Oh, that was bad. Very bad. But he didn't dare make this man any more panicked than he already was. "Your first fire, Specialist?"

"Wha--? Um, yes, sir."

"I've gone through twelve shipboard fires. Eleven of them were put out by the automatic systems. The twelfth was in an FTL tube where the firefighting systems can't be piped—is that what's happening here?"

Delacort nodded.

"I put that one out with a handheld extinguisher, while I was in my damage control rotation. There's hardly anything in those tubes that can burn, and there's never been a case of an engine room exploding because of a fire. So here's what we're going to do: I'm going to walk, in this plain old duty uniform, to engineering. I'm not going to look back—I expect you to follow me."

Delacort swallowed. "Sir ... um, my team ..."

"You leave that to me." Turning, Gage hurried the other way. He didn't look back, but after a pause he heard that muffled thump, from boots covered by fireproof material.

Someday, Gage thought, he might get the hang of this being in charge thing.

He stopped beside a nervous looking crewman, who crouched on the deck in the same silver fire control gear. His helmet was at his feet, ready to go, and the red fire cart waited right beside him, but the door to the engineer section remained firmly closed. "What's the word, Mr. Pimental?"

Pimental looked back, did a double take, and clambered to his feet. "Delacort, what the hell—I thought you were right behind me."

"I accidentally hit my distress button, and he came back to make sure I was okay."

Looking puzzled, Pimental checked the readout on his arm. "But—"

"I guess it only went to him because he was a little closer." Gage looked to the half dozen engineering crewmembers, in their gray duty overalls, who leaned against the gunmetal plastisteel wall. One suppressed a cough; the others, who'd been off duty, looked annoyed. None seemed inclined to argue. "Thank you, Mr. Delacort, but let your partner know what you're doing next time."

Delacort cast a dazed look at him, then turned away. "Yes, sir."

"Okay, so give me a report."

"We have two in from here," Pimental told him. We could see flames when they first went in, but they've signaled it's under control."

"Where's the Chief Engineer?"

"Lt. Brande is still inside, Skipper," said the engineering crewmember with the cough. "It looked bad at first, but he said he's got it handled."

"Lt. Brande should maybe be glad I showed up, and not the Executive Officer." Lieutenant Endo had lately taken to threatening anyone who broke safety regulations with a suit-free trip through the airlock—which was a breach of safety regulations.

Now what? A fire crew was inside, but they weren't dragging Brande out. He could get an update from the damage control officer, but a week ago he'd charged the damage control officer with dereliction of duty and threw thrown off the ship. At least he waited for a shuttle to pick the man up, instead of the quicker method Endo recommended, involving a firing squad.

Still, it was starting to look like Gage's very first disciplinary action had come back to bite him.

The door to the engineering section slid open. Smoke puffed out, and everyone in the corridor recoiled from the acrid smell of burned plastics. But it cleared quickly, until all that was left was a sheet of smoke that seeped through at ceiling level, then rolled up and into the air intake. Two firefighters walked out, their headgear already off, and began pulling off air masks. That was the extent of the excitement, so for the moment all Gage knew was that the environmental filters would have their work cut out for them. "Situation report."

"Fire's out, Skipper." They both got busy pulling off the silvery fire suits, but one paused to jerk a thumb back toward engineering. "It was in the drive mech. Lt. Brande figured you'd be out here, said to send you in. He doesn't think anything's permanently damaged."

"He would know." By the time Gage walked into the small area, all that was left of the smoke was the smell, and black stains that climbed the side of a panel. The panel was set into a long, four feet high tube that ran the length of the room, studded with controls and readouts but otherwise as gray as the rest of the ship. Seriously, the fleet couldn't afford some extra paint? Maybe just highlights? "Gage to bridge. Cancel general quarters. XO, I'd like you down here."

As soon as he spoke, a head and torso rose up from behind the drive tube. Chief Engineer Brande stood at least a full head taller than Gage, and had dark, lined skin that spoke to his years planetside. Rumor had it Brande was full blooded Navajo Indian, which Gage very much doubted, and that Brande used to bench press horses, which Gage very much believed. The man's muscles were about to burst through his coveralls, and the wild disarray of his normally controlled, jet black hair made him appear as though he was about to beat someone.

He looked scared.

"Sir, we don't really need Lt. Endo down here."

"Well, we had a fire, Brande. Get it? Firebrand?"

Brande got on his hands and knees to crawl under the drive tube, then stood beside his captain. "Two days ago she found one of my night crew dozing at his post, and threw him."

"Threw him?"

Brande pointed across engineering. There wasn't much "across", so Gage could easily see a slight dent in a wall panel. "Threw him."

"Is he okay?"

"Physically."

"I'll talk to her." At Brande's concerned look, he added, "From a distance. But you got the joke, right?"

"Firebrand, yessir. It's a good one." Brande didn't even break a smile.

"No it's not, but I appreciate the support." Gage looked around the rest of the engine room. Here, more than anywhere, the ship seemed unfinished: Pipes and ducts crisscrossed the ceiling and now and then ran down the walls, with the majority of them seeming to lead to or from the giant—well, relatively giant—tube that housed most of the FTL drive. "The drive's okay, though? Is Ghost around?"

"It'll have to cool and be cleaned out before we know more. The drive, I mean. Ghost just passed by, then disappeared into the aft bulkhead."

Gage glanced that direction, although he couldn't see Ghost—most people couldn't. "It looked all right, though? Not peaked, or possibly constipated?"

That brought a laugh from Brande. "Looks the same as always, sir: kind of a rainbow hued, shimmering column that hurts when you look straight at it. But as long as there's a Ghost around, the FTL drive is up and functional."

"I can feel when they pass through me. Kind of electrical and cold, at the same time."

"You can? That puts you in rare company, Skipper. Only about three percent of the population can see or feel a Ghost, so they say, and most of those end up engineers."

"My C plus average in the engineering rotation exiled me from that career path, I'm afraid." Still, the Ghosts had always fascinated him. After almost five hundred years, there was still no agreement on what they were. Some manifestation of the FTL drive's ability to breach dimensions? A reaction by some of the more sensitive around a drive's energy waves, causing their minds to hallucinate? Einstein, back from the dead?

"Sometimes ..." Brande hesitated. "Well, some see it and some don't. But I've heard that sometimes, when at FTL drive is damaged and about to break down, that drive's Ghost loses its color and gets even more out of focus. Becomes a blob of gray."

"That's not a spooky thought at all."

They both paused when a female voice rose from out in the hallway. "Why are you all just standing there?"

Turning, Brande busied himself with the fire-scorched panel. They'd both heard the rage in the voice outside.

"The fire is out and you're on duty—get your asses in there or I'll have you outside in a suit, patching micro-meteor spots until the war is over. Maybe *without* a suit."

The engineering crew rushed in, some taking their assigned stations, others cowering beside Brande. "Help me with this," Brande hissed to them. "For spirit's sake, look busy."

Sachiko Endo stalked into the room. She looked the same as always: Black hair layered short so she didn't have to deal with it, navy blue duty coveralls pressed and spotless, hazel eyes flashing, round face full of rage. She looked around for something to hurt.

"Who's minding the store, Sachi?" Gage asked, keeping his voice deliberately mild.

"Lt. Biermann took the con, hopefully not through an alcoholic haze." She crossed her arms. "What happened here?"

"Lt. Biermann's alcohol still exploded." Endo's eyes widened. The engineering crew froze. "Just kidding, his still's in my quarters. Mr. Brande is about to tell us what happened."

"The muffler fell off." Pulling the panel off, Brande set it aside and gestured into the machinery, where the slightest whiff of white vapor puffed out.

"The muffler?" Endo's eyes furrowed and she leaned forward, too surprised to be angry. "The *muffler*?"

"Well, that's what we call it, sir. It's a Syracci invention—the real name's hard to pronounce. They were made standard on Stuart class corvettes, just before the war broke out."

"Do we have spares?" Gage asked.

Brande winced, which pretty much gave Gage his answer. "No, sir. According to the engineers, these things should outlast the expected life of the ship. But it shattered somehow, and we have to dig the pieces out and recheck the systems before we can go back into FTL."

"According to engineers? Syracci engineers?" Endo's voice dropped an octave. Around her, the engineering crew slowly backed away.

"Yes, sir."

"Lt. Brande ... the Syraccians don't like us."

"That's an unfair assessment, XO." Even as he said it, Gage knew he'd made a mistake. His first officer rounded on him, her eyes blazing, so he spoke before she could. "They're our allies, and they're threatened with invasion, too. They just think we're ugly because we look like ... us." He turned to the others, pretending not to hear Endo take in a breath. "Mr. Brande, send the specs for that part to Specialist Fleur. In half an hour I want her and the command staff in the briefing room."

Without waiting for an answer he walked out, with Endo close behind him. He led her through the ship into officer country, strode without hesitation into her quarters, and only turned to her when the door closed behind them. "You need to control your temper."

She drew herself up ... then deflated. "I know."

"Also, you need to stop throwing things against the wall of your quarters late at night." He pointed across the Spartan room to the far wall, where the plastisteel was marred just above her bunk by several marks of uncertain origin, and two dents. Plastisteel didn't dent easily, but she'd managed it four times so far on the *Beowulf.* "My bunk is right on the other side of that bulkhead, and I have trouble sleeping as it is."

"You have trouble sleeping?"

Ah, crap. "We went through that experience together, Sachi. Do you think I spend an hour every night trying to destroy the fitness equipment for my health?"

"Well, yes." The First Officer gazed at him, as if amazed he showed any weakness. "You seem so ..."

"It's an act. We've known each other for ten years, you should have figured that out. I'm an accomplished actor. I once played Hamlet so well he didn't die at the end." Endo smiled, rendering her commander speechless. It completely changed her face, making her look like a teenage schoolgirl. "What? I thought you didn't get my sense of humor."

"You should know better than that. We've known each other for ten years."

Ouch. "Bien jugado." With a sigh, Gage squeezed the bridge of his nose. "You know, all I wanted growing up was to be science officer on a science vessel ... or a least a cruiser."

"All fleet science and research vessels have been pulled for the duration of the war—you'd be out of a job."

"True. They'd have me doing quality control, fitting weapons systems at a shipyard. Okay, make sure engineering gets that mess cleaned up—without tearing off any arms."

For an instant, just a hint of the smile came back. "How about ears?"

"No ears ... well ... a necklace of ears would definitely liven up these coveralls a bit. But no, they'll need those. Half an hour." As he started to walk away, Endo called him.

"Where are you going?"

"Research. We need to get this boat moving again."

"May I remind the captain that we're on a shakedown cruise, headed into a non-combat area?"

Now it was Gage's turn to smile. "Non-combat? Don't be so sure."

He saw her questioning look, but there were things he wasn't prepared to explain to anyone, even her, just yet.

ABOUT THE AUTHOR

Mark R. Hunter is an author, firefighter, humorist, Dad, and self-proclaimed home maintenance failure from northeast Indiana. His first novel, *Storm Chaser*, was published in 2011. Since then he's published a handful of novels, short stories, and nonfiction projects through both traditional publishers and self-publishing. When he's not writing, he likes to write.

ABOUT THE EDITOR

Emily Hunter is Mark's wife, and is an Indiana transplant originally from Southeast Missouri. She got her Bachelor's in English with a writing concentration from Indianan University (IPFW) in 2014. She does the extra, technical, and behind-the-scenes stuff with Mark's writing, along with being a joint author of *Images of America: Albion and Noble County*.

Made in the USA
Lexington, KY
27 April 2015